100 PRAYERS *of a* WRITER

Praise for *100 Prayers of a Writer*

Wade Webster has a gift for approaching the throne of God in prayer with humility and authenticity. His prayers reflect a heart that knows its Savior and trusts Him to provide for every need. If you are looking for a tool to aid you in your own prayer life, consider Wade's book.

"MaryAnn Diorio, PhD, DMin, MFA
Novelist and children's book author
Merchantville, New Jersey"

100 PRAYERS *of a* WRITER

WADE WEBSTER

Copyright 2019 by Author Wade Webster, LLC. All rights reserved.

ISBN Softcover   978-1-951469-11-5

Scriptures taken from the Holy Bible, New International Version, NIV. Copyright 1973, 1978, 1984 by Biblica, Inc. Used by permission of Zondervan, All rights reserved worldwide. www.zondervan.com"

All rights reserved. No part of this book may be reproduced or transmitted in any form or by any means, electronic or mechanical, including photocopying, recording, or by any information storage and retrieval system without express written permission from the author, except in the case of brief quotations embodied in critical reviews and certain other non-commercial uses permitted by copyright law.

Printed in the United States of America.

To order additional copies of this book, contact:
Bookwhip
1-855-339-3589
https://www.bookwhip.com

After I prayed in our adult fellowship at church the prayer I called My Prayer of Surrender, a friend suggested I write prayers. My first thought was, "You don't write prayers, they flow from the heart." Within a year, God opened the door for me to compose these prayers. They began as a weekly offering on the American Christian Fiction Writers' children's fiction e-mail loop. The response of the recipients was so tremendous I knew I needed to make these available to more people. Two years worth of love and worship are before you now.

I dedicate this book to Sue Sullins.

Thank you for planting the seed of writing prayers. May God be glorified and His children be drawn closer to Him by the reading of and meditating on these prayers.

CONTENTS

Suggestions For Using This Book.. 8

My Prayer of Surrender 10

The Spiritual Armor of God 13

The Beatitudes 31

1 Corinthians 13 Love 55

The Fruit of the Spirit 87

The Ten Commandments 109

The I AM Statements of Jesus 131

Times And Seasons 149

The Hall of Faith 169

Psalm 23 209

Prayer Topics 230

SUGGESTIONS FOR USING THIS BOOK

This book of prayers should not be read in one sitting. Each prayer needs to be read deliberately and slowly. If you have the proper solitude, read it out loud. Focus on one per day or week. Leave the book open to that prayer and reread it throughout the day or week. This will train you to remain open to talking with God on a continuous basis. Feel free to read the portion of the Bible for that chapter while you read those prayers. The Bible is God's primary means of communicating to us.

These prayers are not meant to be memorized. I hope they bring you into a habit of talking to God on a regular basis. Too often people aren't comfortable approaching God. I hope you catch the balance of reverence and familiarity God appreciates from His spiritual children. Use a notebook or journal to record things that really speak to you. Write down the personal struggle you're dealing with currently. The next time you work through these prayers you'll be amazed how much you've grown closer to God in your spiritual life.

Although written to a group of writers originally, I did my best to remove references to writing in these prayers. The main theme is a relationship with God the Father. There are a few sentences that couldn't be changed. Please forgive these references and understand where they came from. If they encourage you to write something, all the better. These prayers combine Wade's two main passions: writing and talking to God. He prays that comes through as you experience them.

These prayers don't have to be read in any particular order. Feel free to read them from beginning to end, or read a chapter that appeals to you first. For instance, if you're doing a Bible study on the Fruit of the Spirit you can focus on that chapter without reading the previous prayers. If you are looking for a prayer on peace you can turn to a prayer that focuses on that topic to meditate on.

I hope these prayers mean as much to you as they have to me. Enjoy them purposefully. Your heavenly Father is waiting for you to come to Him now.

Have a great day. Wade Webster

MY PRAYER OF SURRENDER

I give you my life, God, all of it! Please use it as You see fit.

Take my feet. They try to take me places I know I shouldn't go to. Give me Your feet, beautiful feet that go to the hurting and offer hope and help. Feet that flee from the evil that tries so hard to entrap me. As I was reading through the Easter story, I pondered why You washed the disciple's feet. You explained to Peter that only his feet needed to be washed. Why? What's so special about the feet? I realized that their feet collected dust off the streets. I saw the lesson: feet are the part of the body that comes in contact with the world. Help me wash this world's residue off me by reading Your Word on a regular basis. Keep me as pure as I can stay while still reaching people for You. Take my hands. They grab too much stuff; so much so that I can't reach out to anyone when the need arises. As You restored the withered hand, replace my hands with Yours. Attach them to arms that give warm hugs. Give me hands that work for You in all I do.

Take my eyes. They long to linger on things they shouldn't. I'm ashamed to admit that. Pluck them out and give me Your eyes, eyes that look past the surface and see the pain. I long for eyes that shed tears when I watch the evening news. Help me see the solutions to others' problems.

Take my tongue. That muscle in my mouth can be so sharp and bitter. Touch my tongue and give me one that's quick to encourage and build others up. Come to think of it, You explained that the words that come out of my mouth originate in my heart. So…

Take my heart. I was taught in school that it's only a muscle that pumps blood. But I think it's been a gradual callousing that has caused it to become a heart of stone. Give me a soft heart that longs to delight myself in You so I can discover the desires You have for me.

Take my entire being and fill it with Your Word. Let me use it as my compass to find my way on the straight and narrow path. May I be a light that guides lost souls to You with just enough salt to cause a thirst for Your love. Use me to show others the way to Your throne and kingdom for all eternity.

I ask this in Jesus's precious name. Amen

THE SPIRITUAL ARMOR OF GOD

EPHESIANS 6:13-14A

Therefore put on the full armor of God....
Stand firm then, with the belt of truth
buckled around your waist.

Dear Heavenly Father,

I come to You, the Author of all truth, in a desperate search for answers. The world I live in is full of failed directions and dead ends. You are the only source of truth: full, meaningful honesty. I long for Your answers in this turbulent, adversarial place I find myself in. Keep me on the narrow path of truth.

The broad road is much more popular, but You told me its end is destruction. Remind me of that fact whenever I veer off the course You set for me. I need to remain pure and unblemished to be most useful for Your work. Remind me of the urgency to wash this world off my feet. Hold me in the holy way for You.

Our culture says truth is different for everybody. Nobody has all the right answers. Everybody knows better than that deep down. The only reason they convince themselves of that is so they can do whatever pleases their selfish desires. Mine isn't a popularity contest, I live for an audience of one. Enable me for the great pleasure of You.

The vocal minority tells me the Bible is full of fables and fiction. I call it Your Word because I know You inspired the authors with the words You want me to hear. Your truth is open for everybody. Even if the majority of people never read Your book for themselves, I'll cherish every second I can spend with it. Starve me for an intense desire for You.

A hunger and thirst is my request. Fulfill these needs with the only source that truly satisfies. Your truths are what everybody longs for. Give me the means to share this message with those around me. I don't want to hoard the answers for myself while others flounder in emptiness. Enrich me with only honest words for everyone.

The Easter season is when I remember the ultimate sacrifice You made to secure my eternal security with You. Help me to never forget the message we all need. You love us so much You gave Your Son for everybody. That is the ultimate truth I must be willing to die for. Anoint me for my sacrificial service for You.

It's in the name of the One who agonized in the garden yet fulfilled His mission for me, Jesus Christ, I come to You with my desires. Amen

EPHESIANS 6:13, 14B

Therefore put on the full armor of God,
with the breastplate of righteousness in place.

Dear Heavenly Father,

I come to You in awe and wonder after the stark reminder of Your incredible love for me as I remembered another Easter. That first Easter was too incredible for anyone to comprehend, even though they were there as witnesses. Don't let me forget the excitement they lived through. Remind me often of Your awesomeness.

As I think of Your armor I'm called to wear, I come to the breastplate, that article that protects the vital organs in my chest. The lungs put oxygen in the blood, and the heart pumps that essential element throughout my body. Without either one, I would die rather quickly. Protect me constantly with Your care.

Righteousness is merely the act of being right. In my own strength, I know I can't be right very often. I call upon Your provision of correct thinking to bring me into this state of truth. Help me see things from Your perspective. My outlook is too skewed by the culture I live in. Guide me prayerfully with Your thoughts.

You became one of us once. You lived a life I need to emulate. You showed me how to treat others: with respect, dignity, and love. I try in my own desire but come up short too often. Thank You for coming into me by Your Spirit to give me the correct attitude I need to share Your love with fellow travelers. Empower me daily with Your desires.

I'm too blinded by this world I live in to be very useful to You. Give me the right attitude, right desire, right motive, right thoughts, and most of all, the right deeds to show Your love to those around me. I so long to reach others with Your love. Use me as You see fit to open the eyes of those in my path. Employ me today as Your mouthpiece.

I often forget that those who don't know You are living lives of reckless self-preservation. They're merely seeking happiness in any form they can find. Help me not to judge them too quickly but empathize with them. Remind me that I too was in their shoes not long ago. Focus my heart on the cause.

It's in the name of the One who died and rose again, Jesus Christ, that I pray. Amen

EPHESIANS 6:13, 15

Therefore put on the full armor of God, with your feet fitted with the readiness that comes from the gospel of peace.

Dear Heavenly Father,

I come before Your throne in total awestruck wonder. There is none who can ever match Your power and might. Yet You love me with an immensely powerful love. You came to earth as one of us to give me an example to live by and a sacrifice to cling to. Your promise is to never leave me. I give You my utmost.

As I continue to put Your armor on, I come to the protection for the feet. My feet come in contact with the world. This world must always be washed off my feet to keep me pure. Remind me of that so I don't become mired in its mud. Keep me on Your path for my life, not sidetracked by what I see. I give You my heart.

You ask me to remain always ready. Give me words fitly spoken. Lead me to those who need comfort. Guide me to people in search of Your truth, even if they don't know that's what they're seeking.

Help me fit Your word into conversations so You are made known as the only answer to life's dilemmas. I give You my tongue.

You are the good news everyone needs to hear about. Your gospel will bring peace to yearning souls. You are the missing piece others require but haven't found. Use me to bring that good news to those around me. Give me words that tell that news so grand and precious. I give You my words.

Peace is such a popular concept on this planet. Yet it remains the most elusive goal to attain. Wars are ironically fought in a desire to obtain peace. You paid the ultimate price to bring us peace, but pride keeps this at a distance from the majority of people. Use me to present Your peace to all. I give you my life.

Your Word promises a peace that surpasses understanding. Those of us who have experienced that peace know how fleeting it is in this life. It's only a foretaste of our future with You. That must be why it's the ultimate goal for everybody. It's that part of creation that was lost in Eden. I give You my destiny.

Give me beautiful feet that carry Your truth and peace to the hurting souls around me. Help people see Your peace in me so they ask how they can get that same yearning fulfilled. Protect me from the enemy's forces as I carry out Your will on this battleground called earth. I give You my soul.

I acknowledge I can come to You only in the name of Jesus Christ. Amen

EPHESIANS 6:13, 16

Therefore put on the full armor of God,
take up the shield of faith, with which you can
extinguish all the flaming arrows of the evil one.

Dear Heavenly Father,

As the Creator of everything from nothing, I stand in amazement that You even want me to talk to You. Your power is unmatched. Your holiness is unparalleled. Your justice is immense. Yet Your love for me is so overwhelming I stand in awe that You desire my time and attention. I come to You amazed.

I acknowledge that on my own I could never stand a chance of escaping Your judgment because of my sinfulness. It's only because of Your indescribable gift of love lavished on me by Jesus Christ's death and resurrection that I can take advantage of Your incredible love of a Father. I bow before You humbled.

As I continue to prepare for my spiritual battle, I take up my shield. This mobile piece of equipment can be used to protect different parts as needed. When we stand side by side, our shields can interlock and become a formidable barrier for the enemy forces. I stand before You ready.

Faith is the material this equipment is made of— nothing visible, but believed. Just because we can't see it doesn't mean it isn't real. Faith in You can be more of a force than anything man-made. Strengthen my faith like you did for David who fought off lions and bears before he faced Goliath. I ask for Your courage.

The enemy doesn't fight fair. His flaming arrows come in many forms: discouragement, fear, envy, hate, pride, lust, greed, the list could fill a book. Give me Your eyes to see the truth of my circumstances. Remind me that I'm on the winning side no matter what the outlook appears to be now. I long for Your vision.

The gravity of this world pulls me down. It saps my energy and drains my reserves. Renew in me a right spirit to maintain the work You've given me to do. I'm so easily distracted by things around me. Keep my eyes on what's important. Remind me how this battle is Yours. I thirst for Your sustenance.

I delight in You, Father. Your love compels me to give my best to Your service. My desires have been given to me by You. Use my words to declare Your love to everyone. Keep me grounded in the truth so I present it honestly in a way people will understand and embrace. I hunger for Your assignments.

I come to You by the gracious name of Jesus Christ, my Lord and Savior. Amen

EPHESIANS 6:13, 17A

Therefore put on the full armor of God,
take the helmet of salvation.

Dear Heavenly Father,

I come again into Your presence amazed. I'm astounded that You want me to come to You. Why do You enjoy my company? Because that's the reason You created me in the first place. You'd love nothing more than for me to love You. So I come in obedience and in adoration of You. Welcome me into Your presence.

My armor today is the helmet. That head covering is essential to keeping me safe in battle. My brain is vital yet vulnerable. A simple piece of shrapnel can end a soldier's life in an instant. A helmet made of the right material can deflect such injury and keep me in the battle. Protect me with Your power.

My mind is under so much attack these days. My eyes see things they shouldn't. My ears hear things that I know better to let them listen to. My nose can even smell things that take my mind to places it shouldn't go to. My mouth joins in conversations that drag me down. Help me guard my purity.

To counter these attacks, I need Your refreshment. Give me a deep desire to fill my mind with Your truths. Give me a distaste for what this world has to offer. Its short-term pleasures leave me empty. Remind me that You are saving Your best for last. My eternal home will be magnificent. Entice me with Your promises.

Salvation is what our spiritual helmets are made of. Jesus Christ is the only source of this wealth. It's only because of His great sacrifice for me that I can even contemplate this relationship with You. Your Word promises me that You'll never leave me nor forsake me. That truth will keep me strong. Steady me with this truth.

I am now covered from the soles of my feet to the top of my head and stand ready for my marching orders. I already have a desire to write. Please give me worthwhile stories that the Holy Spirit can use to convince people of Your love for them also. Your words for today's people are what I want. Use me as Your scribe.

The enemy is still seeking any vulnerability he can find in me. Keep me strong in this battle. Help me remember I am on the winning side. Satan will not win, but that doesn't mean he'll just give up. The attacks will only strengthen against me as his time draws to a close. Encourage me to keep fighting.

I ask these things in the mighty name of Jesus Christ. Amen

EPHESIANS 6:13, 17B

Therefore put on the full armor of God, take the sword of the Spirit, which is the Word of God.

Dear Heavenly Father,

I approach Your throne of grace as a child coming to my Daddy to share my life with. I owe my life to You, both my spiritual and physical life. Your power has established this divine hierarchy with You as the head and me as the dependent one. I feel Your smile as I come.

This relationship has been firmly established by Jesus's death and resurrection. I acknowledge this is the only way I can come to You. I'm grateful You long for my time and attention. Help me not take this relationship for granted. Give me a mutual longing to be with You. I need Your love as I live.

As I prepare for the spiritual battle before me, I'm finally given a weapon to use, a sword. This isn't a general tool to be used at a distance in battle. No, this implement requires close-quarters combat. I can't expect to be able to deftly use this sword without practice. I require Your training as I fight.

This sword is Your Word, the Bible. It's not enough that I own a Bible and expect to be able to fight off the enemy. No, I need to make Your Word a part of my very being to be able to utilize this weapon to its full potential. Help me feed my soul with the nourishment that comes from intake. I relish Your words as I breathe.

Give me a serious hunger and thirst for Your truths. I need to grow in my walk every day. As muscles grow from constant use, give me a familiarity with the Bible that makes me stand out to those around me. It should show in my life that I'm different from those who don't know You. I reflect Your light as I shine.

Improper use of a weapon can cause more harm than good. Help me use Your word in the right way. Don't let me harm Your work with my carelessness. Use Your Holy Spirit to guide me in the correct use of truth. Lead me to good teachers who long to implant the right instruction. I beseech Your wisdom as I operate.

The enemy loves to twist Your word to fit his schemes. Give me the discernment to detect this deception. Use me to point out these lies as I come across them. Guide my words as I use them to reach others for You. Help me avoid the snares set up to trap me away from Your work for me. I desire Your discretion as I live.

It's in the matchless name of Jesus Christ I come to You now. Amen

EPHESIANS 6:18, 19A, 20B

And pray in the Spirit on all occasions with
all kinds of prayers and requests. With this in mind,
be alert and always keep on praying for all the saints.
Pray also for me, pray that I may declare
the gospel fearlessly, as I should.

Dear Heavenly Father,

I come to Abba on my knees. A father's love and compassion is what I need. Grace and forgiveness are what You offer me. It's more than I deserve, but Your heart's cry is for me to trust You. You bridged this divide between Your holiness and my filthy sinfulness by coming as the sacrifice I need. Your love is amazing.

I utilize the final portion of our soldier's equipment now as I speak to You. A lot of messages on the full armor of God stop before they get to this plea from Paul to pray. He mentions it in verb form at least four times in three verses, so it must be extremely important to me in my battle. Your access is remarkable.

I'm called upon to pray in the Spirit because You are Spirit. A portion of each human has this spiritual essence in us to breech this chasm. Help me develop this habit so it becomes as natural to me as breathing. As Your Spirit is alive in me, Your child, use it to draw me into communion with You. Your presence is life-giving.

Paul tells me to use all kinds of prayers in speaking to You. Give me the trust to delve into my darkest places I hide from others as I call on You. You know what I'm made of anyway. There's nothing that's hidden from Your sight. So help me to cry out and spiritually bleed as I expose my pain when needed. Your intimacy is awesome.

I'm told to pray for others. This intercessory aspect of prayer is something that shouldn't be taken lightly. Help me see the honest needs of others so I can intelligently ask for guidance from You in how I can help. Give me wisdom to know when I need to step back and wait on You for a response. Your counsel is humbling.

Help me to declare Your gospel fearlessly. Use my words to lead people to this intimacy with the Holy God that I embrace. This is too good to hoard for myself. Use me to reach others. Remind me that it's not me being rejected when they turn away from the truth, but You. Your orders are serious.

Since this battle is on the spiritual realm, it makes sense that I should be able to call on Your assistance for victory. As our human military can call for air strikes to assist ground fighters, help me call in spiritual combatants to aid me in my warfare. Thank You for this backup. Your assistance is appreciated.

It's all because of what Jesus accomplished that prayer is even possible. Thank You. Amen

EPHESIANS 6:10-20

Dear Heavenly Father,

I come to you with my mouth held open. You thought of everything to help me survive the spiritual assault on my life. A warrior is nothing without protection. You really do want me to succeed. Thank You for supplying.

My belt that holds weapons is a central part of my uniform. There's no better material than truth to hold all I need in this life. Life is senseless without truth. Shifting sand holds nothing. Thank You for Your wisdom.

A metal breastplate gives better protection than a bare chest. A righteous, godly life is the greatest source of protection for my heart. Once the enemy reaches the heart, the battle is over. Thank You for preserving.

Many battles are averted because of peace. Help me carry this virtue wherever I go. It must begin with peace with You, Father. Use me to deliver that message to as many others as possible. Thank You for providing.

I can stand in Your service because I know You will never leave me. My faith has grown from hard lessons in my life. I can divert whatever comes my way by remembering that fact. You are always there for me. Thank You for sustaining.

You only provided one offensive weapon for me. But when it's as powerful as Your word, I need nothing else. Help me use it as deftly as Jesus did in His lonely wilderness battle with Satan. Thank You for Your word.

I can't see all the attacks coming my way. The spirit world is beyond my senses. That's why I need the ability to call on Your reinforcements at times. Prayer for myself and others is vital for victory. Thank You for being there.

It's only because of the power of the One who overcame and will ultimately reign, Jesus Christ, I come before you now. Amen

THE BEATITUDES

MATTHEW 5:3

Blessed are the poor in spirit,
for theirs is the kingdom of Heaven.

Dear Heavenly Father,

I acknowledge Your superiority over all things and every living being. Without Your constant attention on creation all that I know would fall apart and I'd be totally lost. Thank You for being such a solid base for me to build my foundation on. Thank You for creating me.

I come to You with a spirit in need of help. My culture tells me all I have to do is think of what I want and I can achieve it. I know better than that. I declare my dependence on You for my next breath and all of my future plans. Thank You for loving me.

You gave each of us a unique spirit, some call them personalities. You're no "cookie-cutter" creator; even different animals within a species have special personalities. Help me use my uniqueness to tell others of Your glory by focusing people's attention on You and Your love. Thank You for personalizing me.

I fall to my knees as I see my shortcomings when I compare myself to Your holiness. I quickly see I can never be in Your presence with all of my stains and sins. You knew I'd need a savior to come and stand in the gap to fill this chasm I'd never be able to cross. Thank You for saving me.

What can I offer You in return for such compassion? How can I ever hope to repay You for giving me Your all on the cross? You drained Your very life blood just so I could come into Your family. I grant You the highest place in my life. Desire me with a conviction to give my all to You. Thank You for equipping me.

In exchange for my commitment to You by declaring my dependence on You, You promise me Your kingdom. How incredibly remarkable You are to place me in Your throne room. What other god would be so generous? There's none that I know of. Thank You for preparing me.

Remind me there are forces at work around me. They want nothing more than to make me fail in my attempts to get Your words out to reach more people with Your offer of hope and love. I know You'll give me assistance on the spiritual realm as needed to aid me in my assignments. Thank You for reinforcing me.

It's in the matchless name of Jesus, the One who gave His all, that I come to You now. Amen

MATTHEW 5:4

Blessed are those who mourn,
for they will be comforted.

Dear Heavenly Father,

I thank You for understanding me to the point that You know I'll mourn at some point in my life. There's always something for me to feel remorse for. Be it a personal relationship gone bad, health issues that hinder me, or a catastrophe I know about. Tears are inevitable for me.

My struggles are not easy for a reason. You're teaching me through them. Help me catch Your lessons so I can become a better person, more like Jesus. Then help me bring my newfound wisdom to others in an understanding way so they can gain from my pain. Lessons are invaluable for me.

Sadness is not a comfortable place for me. I long to be happy. I want to see everybody happy. But that state of perfection can never happen in this sin-filled world. Selfish tendencies make some abuse their happiness at the expense of others. Pain is inherent to me.

I'll never understand true comfort if I never feel true pain. My view of comfort is in direct proportion with my experience with hurt. Help me see how much I feel the pain of others by my own personal dealings with anguish. Give me Your eyes as I look at others. Compassion is needed by me.

You promise me comfort in this verse. I must first use my experiences to comfort those who are experiencing similar pain. As I reach out with my arms, I receive a new level of comfort for my own hurt. Your love is best expressed through me to this aching world. Comfort is returned to me.

Ultimately, the only true comfort I'll ever hope to experience will only be found when I reach my eternal home, heaven. Remind me this world is not my home. I get so transfixed on my surroundings that I forget that fact. Homecoming is anticipated by me.

Satan will continue to tell me this life is all about finding my own happiness. He twists the truth to get me to lose my focus. Keep me aligned with You. I need to do what You have for me. Guide me in that plan. Refocus is required of me.

I come to You by the only true source of comfort, Jesus Christ. Amen

MATTHEW 5:5

Blessed are the meek, for they
will inherit the earth.

Dear Heavenly Father,

I am awestruck by Your power. You who created everything out of nothing and can end it all in a thought. Yet You yearn for me to commune with You. You long to call me Your own. A personal relationship is Your ultimate desire. You've given each person a void that only You can fill. Bring me to Your Self.

Your holy perfection is unmatched. I can never hope to reach You on my own effort. That's why You stepped into my world in the form of a helpless baby as You became one of us. Your ultimate goal was to become the ultimate sacrifice for me so I can come to You. Complete me with Your Son.

You promise me Your Holy Spirit so I can tap into Your power to help me become more like Jesus Christ. This lifelong journey needs to be taken one step at a time. Give me the patience and grace to grow as near to Your Son's reflection as I can on this earth. Empower me with Your Spirit.

Meekness is the watchword for today. This isn't the politically correct message of my day. I'm told to push my way to the top, position myself to the next level of power until I succeed. Your message is quite the opposite. You tell me to humble myself and become small. Teach me with Your Word.

Help me stoop down to help those who can't help me in return, just like Jesus did. Give me the grace to look past my prejudices in order to show Your strength. A servant is what You're calling me to be. Grant me a heart that looks into the pain of others and propels me to action. Break me with Your love.

The spiritual warfare I face is unrelenting. The closer I am to being who You want me to be, the stronger the attacks become. Satan doesn't want me to get Your message out, so he'll do his best to stop me. Remind me that in the end, we win. I will inherit the earth with Jesus as my King. Embolden me with Your mission.

I ask this in the precious name of Jesus Christ, the epitome of meekness and power. Amen

MATTHEW 5:6

Blessed are those who hunger and thirst for righteousness, for they will be filled.

Dear Heavenly Father,

My Creator and Sustainer who designed me to hunger and thirst in a physical way to manifest my spiritual reality that I can't see. Thank You for caring for me to the point of giving me this personal means to show me my need for You. This proves that You didn't simply create me then turn Your back on me. Thank You for Your love.

Everybody has this intrinsic desire that can only be filled by You; they just don't recognize where to slake this thirst. They try all the cover- up options laid out by our society. Give me ways to draw them in and present You in a way that appeals to their common sense and shows Your love. Thank You for my life.

This spiritual hunger is mistakenly filled in physical ways by unknowing people who haven't heard Your message of sacrificial love. Their search for ultimate truth isn't even what they recognize they need. Give me the words that show the path to You through Your Son, Jesus Christ. Thank You for this truth.

Of course, my attempts will be useless without the working of the Holy Spirit in others' lives. I pray for Your revelation to occur as people see my efforts to the point of making an eternal impact on their hearts. Introduce me to those who are touched when we all get to heaven. Thank You for this hope.

The filling mentioned in this verse will be the Holy Spirit's role to take. The God-shaped void in every person will be satisfied only when God is made intimately real to the individual. Use me to show the way to You, not only with my words, but with the life I live daily. Thank You for this impact.

Satan will do everything he possibly can to keep me from my mission. His distractions may even be disguised as useful things that will benefit others in some way. He may also cause havoc in my life to sidetrack me. Help me to overcome any obstacles I face to fulfill my calling. Thank You for Your assistance.

I come to You only in the name of Jesus Christ, the One who fed the multitudes. Amen

MATTHEW 5:7

Blessed are the merciful, for they
shall be shown mercy.

Dear Heavenly Father,

    Having been to Moore, Oklahoma, for two days of tornado cleanup, I hold a fresh vision of Your power. The total devastation of an entire neighborhood was completely breathtaking. Then I realized this wasn't even the tip of Your smallest finger coming down to brush our tiny planet. Your awesomeness is enormous.

    A strip of houses six blocks wide is completely wiped out. Trees don't even have their bark on them. Vehicles are wrapped around trees. Where is Your mercy in all this? I saw it in the family whose lot we cleared as they came by in the afternoon to claim their belongings we found in the rubble. Your mercy is mysterious.

    They have each other as they rebuild their lives and try to find their new normal. The stuff is just stuff now. Replaceable artifacts will never be found. Life will go on because of Your mercy. The heirloom necklace we found is still held dear by them, as are some of the boys' toys (a slingshot and a globe). Your providence is mind-boggling.

Of course, there are those who didn't survive the storm this time. Their time to accept Jesus as their Savior is gone. You have some of them with You now. Others are lost for eternity. Help me grasp the urgency of this uncertain life I live here. Your commission to me is to make disciples. Your edict is established.

Now that I have my marching orders, help me go forth and proclaim Your truth in as many ways as I can. Help me live a life that draws people to You. Use my words to open minds and hearts to see their need for You through Jesus Christ. Break me to the point of new priorities in life. Your redemption is eternal.

I saw You there as we drove around. You were in the many churches that had stockpiles of bottled water and various supplies for people affected by this disaster. This outreach is bringing people to You in remarkable ways. Souls are being saved. Eternal destinies are being changed because of Your mercy. Your love is apparent.

Satan is also at work there. Depression is merely one of his flaming darts. He'll focus some on their loss and the past to pull them away from Your hope and truth. I pray for a strengthening of Your Spirit's work as a revival is taking root in Oklahoma. Help us fan that flame to spread it everywhere. Your future is bright.

It's in the mighty name of Jesus Christ, the One who showed mercy by taking my death sentence on the cross, that I come to Your throne. Amen

MATTHEW 5:8

Blessed are the pure in heart, for they will see God.

Dear Heavenly Father,

I come to You with my earthly father fresh on my mind. For those blessed with godly dads, I thank You for them. An example of You is what is suggested in this physical relationship. That's an awesome assignment to carry out. I appreciate the ones who take this task to heart. Thank You for our dads.

A father is what You want me to call You. I give my devotion and reverence to You as the giver of my life. I turn to You for guidance and answers for my unending questions. I unashamedly give my reliance for my very life to You. I crawl in Your lap for comfort when I'm hurting. Thank You for this intimacy.

In order to see You, I'm called upon to have a pure heart. This is impossible in my own efforts. My heart is so selfish. I find it difficult to focus on others. My first response is too often: "What's in this for me?" I come to my Abba in utter dependence. Create in me a pure heart, oh Lord. Thank You for this assistance.

Give me a heart that breaks when I watch the evening news. Help me respond to the hurting souls around me. Use me in ways I don't even imagine at this time. Motivate me to action by the aching You place in my heart. Let my longing be to help without receiving anything in return. Thank You for this desire.

This whole notion of giving without receiving cuts so cross-cultural. I'm told to look out for number one—me. Shine Your light through me to show the world how Your peace is given when I give myself to others. Give them a desire to seek what makes me tick so I can introduce them to You. Thank You for this opportunity.

The ultimate example of giving myself completely was shown when Jesus gave his very life on the cross. The end result was the possibility of having an intimate relationship between the perfectly Holy God and utterly sinful man. Remind me of this purity of motive as I live out my Christianity. Thank You for this sacrifice.

Distractions are all around me in this battle for purity. Give me the focus I need to succeed in this daily struggle. Keep me grounded in Your Word as I face each assignment I receive. Keep my heart purely guided by Your calling on my life. Bring me a resolve to live for You alone. Thank You for this drive.

I come to Your Holy throne of grace by Jesus's ultimate sacrifice. Amen

MATTHEW 5:9

Blessed are the peacemakers, for they
will be called sons of God.

Dear Heavenly Father,

    I fall before Your throne of grace in reverential fear. Your power and might will never be matched by anyone. Your majesty and dominion cannot be overcome by another. You hold my entire existence in Your thoughts. Without You, I am nothing. Your love for me is the reason You created me. I drop to my knees before You.

    You call me to make peace in this turbulent world I live in. As Satan gets more people to focus on themselves, this request becomes more difficult. As much as it depends on me, I will reach out to make peace. I ask for Your assistance with others.

    I seek a pure heart and motives as I carry out this assignment. Give me the wisdom to know when I must not back down to someone just to keep the peace. There are lines that must not be crossed but defended. I plead for Your wisdom in battle.

Use me to reach between parties at odds with each other. Guide me to show them how they need each other so they can look past their differences to work together. Give me the courage to step in to bring about lasting peace where I can. I come to You for encouragement.

My desire is to be Your instrument of peace, Father. Stretch me out of my comfort zone to obtain this distinction. Help me be the reflection of Your Son in this dark world. Let His light shine through me as I tackle this assignment. I'm honored to be Your mouthpiece.

The father of lies will do his best to stop me from bringing peace to his realm. Give me the strength to overcome his efforts to thwart my attempts. Bind him and his dominion so I can bring Your peace to hearts one at a time. I require from You new boldness.

It's in the mighty name of Him who overcame death and this world's forces, Jesus Christ, that I come to You with these needs. Amen

MATTHEW 5:10

Blessed are those who are persecuted because of righteousness, for theirs is the kingdom of heaven.

Dear Heavenly Father,

I come before Your throne on my knees acknowledging my dependence on You. You created me for a purpose. You have a plan for me. You've equipped me with unique gifts and experiences. Use me as You will.

Those of us who live in countries where we can openly worship You are grateful for such freedom. Give me the courage and determination to use my freedom to present Your amazing gift of grace to all. Empower me as You purpose.

As I'm reminded of those in parts of the world where You are an object of derision, use me to plead to You for their lives. Families are too often torn apart in an attempt to silence Your message of love and forgiveness. Hear me as You desire.

Break my heart to the point of taking any action I can to help my hurting spiritual family members. When I can, let me send financial support to those who are in a position to help near the front battle lines. Embolden me to take action.

Open my eyes to the persecution going on around me. Public schools are placing You in a position of scorn and rejection to our youth. Give me actions that give them hope and courage to stand up for You. Infuse me as You will.

I plead for those doing the persecuting now. Forgive them, Father, they don't really understand what they're doing. They're following those around them in an attempt to fit in. Open their eyes to reality. Enlighten them with Your truth.

Satan is their father of lies. He has too many people believing his twisted schemes. He knows his time is short. He also knows he won't win in the end. Thwart his plans as You will to bring the truth to many. Establish Your kingdom as dominant.

It's in the name of Jesus, the future King, I bring these requests to You. Amen

MATTHEW 5:11-12

Blessed are you when people insult you, persecute
you and falsely say all kinds of evil against you because
of me. Rejoice and be glad, because great is your reward
in heaven, for in the same way they persecuted
the prophets who came before you.

Dear Heavenly Father,

I bow before Your throne in humble submission, You who created everything with a word. A thought from You brought all I see into existence. Your love has brought me into Your family now. I call You my Father, the one who gave me life and longs to give me all I need to succeed. I acknowledge Your omnipotence.

These verses remind me that not everybody looks at You the same way. Many actually take the opposite stance when they learn of You. They spit in Your face. They do all they can to show they don't need You. Their selfishness is led by the father of lies whom they choose to believe. I acknowledge their choice.

To get back at You, they'll come after Your children. I should expect to receive their insults and attacks. Hopefully they see

You in me. Strengthen me to take these persecutions as badges of honor. It won't be easy to do, but I know You'll never leave me nor forsake me. I acknowledge this battle.

I thank You for giving me this advanced warning that this will happen to me. In this way, I can brace for these jabs. Grant me wisdom to deal with people who attack me to get at You. Give me the right words to counter their attacks so they still see Your love shining through me. I acknowledge my need.

My actions and words go into the world guided by You. Send my words to those who need to hear it most, even if it offends them at first. Your Spirit can open their eyes to Your truth even if that truth wounds them. Give me the words You want sent out. I acknowledge my source.

My e-mails, my Facebook posts, even my tweets are instruments in Your hands to bring a balm of healing to hurting souls. I thank You for counting me worthy to be used by You in this way. I know You don't need me, but You choose to use me as the broken vessel that I am. I acknowledge my dependence.

Satan will do all he can to stop me from completing my mission. He'll use his followers to try to discourage me from sending Your words out to the world. Strengthen me to continue even when it appears nobody is responding to what I send out. Give me the determination to continue following Your call. I acknowledge my assignments.

I bow again before You in the name of Jesus Christ. Amen

MATTHEW 5:13

You are the salt of the earth. But if the salt looses its saltiness, how can it be made salty again? It's no longer good for anything, except to be thrown out and be trampled by men.

Dear Heavenly Father,

I bow before Your throne of grace in humble submission. Your awesome power is too much for me to understand. I'll never have all my questions answered on this earth. I trust You'll continue to hold everything together by Your will. You have a plan for me. Guide me by Your wisdom.

You've called me to be salt, a seemingly benign substance upon first glance. Its properties are very unique. It brings out the flavor of whatever food I add it to, unless I add too much. Help me know when You want me to flavor those around me with Your love. Use me by Your design.

Salt is also used as a preserving agent as it protects food from the harmful effects of decay. I've seen in the Bible how often You delay judging a nation because of the efforts of one person. Give me the spine I need to stand up to what is wrong in my nation so we can continue to glorify You. Strengthen me for Your battle.

Give me words that flavor my world with Your truth. My society has lost its way. Many are thirsting for anything to quench them. May I have the fortitude to show enough of You to bring people to You. Give me words that guide people to Your kingdom. Entrust me with Your truth.

Strengthen me to remain pure for Your service. Don't let me succumb to Satan's traps and give in to my temporary desires for my own selfish pleasure. Keep me focused on the prize of Your upward calling. Give me an eternal view when I become weak and susceptible to failing and falling. Ground me in Your plan.

The last thing I want is to become another casualty along the road of Christian servants who failed. Help me keep my saltiness in this tasteless world. It's too easy for me to lose my purpose and merely entertain, therefore failing to salt anyone. Give me a life that stands out for You. Help me take Your stance.

Satan longs to lull me into complacency. He'll let me gain honor and favor of men if he believes I'll fall away from my original desire to be used by You to reach others. Focus me like a laser to what You've called me to be, a ready instrument for Your glory and honor. Inhabit me as Your puppet.

I ask this in the name of Jesus, the only One who can quench every thirst. Amen

MATTHEW 5:14-16

You are the light of the world. A city on a hill cannot be hidden. Neither do people light a lamp and put it under a bowl. Instead they put it on its stand, and it gives light to everyone in the house. In the same way, let your light shine before men, that they may see your good deeds and praise your Father in heaven.

Dear Heavenly Father,

I'm drawn to You, the Father of light. In You there is no darkness at all. That's what attracts me to You. That's what I need to show others groping along in this dark world we call home. The creation account begins with light. In the new heaven, I'm promised there won't even be any shadows. Shine Your light on me.

You've given me the responsibility to continue to be a beacon of hope. I can merely be a dim reflection of Jesus's perfect light, but I'll do the best I can to guide others home to You. Help me develop an inner light on a personal level so it shines brighter every day. Shine Your light in me.

Help me look past my own inadequacies as I carry out my task of reaching others. Come to think of it, I don't even feel I deserve Your gift of salvation to begin with. Give me the courage to fulfill my purpose You called me to. Use me in spite of my shortcomings and weaknesses. Shine Your light by me.

One way You've equipped me to shine Your light in this dark world is with my life. Sometimes I feel like I'm waiting for a purpose so I can shine Your message to the world in some way. Let me not be so narrow-minded that I think there's only one way You have for me. Shine Your light through me.

Open opportunities that surprise me to anything You have in store for me. Keep me alert to places where I can shine Your light in small ways to touch hearts and lives. Help me develop a voice people want to follow to You. Shine Your light with me.

Satan will do all he can to darken the light You've given me. I ask for Your wisdom as I deal with these distractions and doubts. Give me the courage to step into places I've felt led to go but will stretch me. Help me trust You are the One doing the stretching to broaden your light that I cast. Shine Your light around me.

I ask this in the name of Jesus Christ, the One who is the light. Amen

1 CORINTHIANS 13 LOVE

1 CORINTHIANS 13:4

Love is patient.

Dear Heavenly Father,

You are the creator of love. You made all I see so you could have someone to share Your love with. There are so many things in this world that confuse me, like why is there so much evil? I know love is the most attractive quality anyone can have. So why don't more people try to reach out in love? What is there about wickedness that so many find hard to avoid? Grow me wise.

You give me a definition of love in Your Word that is quite all-encompassing. At least You didn't make me wait for the trait of patience in this list. It seems to be the most endearing quality I find in others, but I discover it's hard to practice in my own life. I thank You for Your patience toward me. I would have given up on me many times by now. Grow me long.

Give me a long- term perspective for my life. I seldom look past the here and now. Give me Your eyes that maintain an eternal view. I have a propensity to want to get past a problem and go on to the next thing in my life. You want to use my problems as teaching lessons. Help me see the changes You want me to make. Bring me into a deeper relationship with You through Jesus. Transform me into His image. Grow me deep.

Give me the patience to grow slowly, like an oak tree. I long to be able to endure life's storms and still be standing. Use me to shelter others from the heat and provide food for their souls so they can continue on. Help me see the futility in growing quickly so I don't have the substance needed to maintain my footing during the hard times. Grow me strong.

Help me wait for others. Sometimes they can't keep up with me; slow me down for them. Often their agenda is different than mine; show me their perspective. Frequently they're going a direction away from me; grant me the grace to let them go. Many walked away from Jesus as He collected followers. Grow me gracious.

It's because of Jesus's patient love for me I pray this. Amen

1 CORINTHIANS 13:4

Love is kind.

Dear Heavenly Father,

    I come to You again as a little child in search of direction from one who is greater than me. Your guidance is unmatched. Your omniscience is complete. Please give me the wisdom and discernment I need to cope in this fallen world. Break my heart at what breaks Your heart. Use me unconditionally.

    Grant me the courage to reach out to my neighbors in kindness. That doesn't mean I'm to reach out to them in the same kind of way they reach out to me. No, use me as Christ's ambassador to show His unconditional love to all. Use me authentically.

    Give me eyes that see needs and act on them before a request for help is made. Help me help the needy. Give me arms that reach around broken hearts with warm hugs. Let others be surprised by my efforts. Use me keenly.

    Lead my beautiful feet to take my hands to the work that isn't being done so I can impact the world for good. Your kindness in love is what this world so desperately needs. You've called me to be Your soldier in this battlefield. Guide me to Your chosen assignments for me in Your timing. Use me warmly.

Guard my tongue from saying hurtful things. Stop me from following my own prideful, painful tendencies to lash out in anger during a discussion or argument. May Your kindness overrule my nature so I can be an instrument of peace. Use me wisely.

I plead for the growth I need to become more like Jesus Christ each moment of my life. May those around me see the difference You make when I give control of my life to You. Let me stand out as different. Use me boldly.

Remind me of the times Jesus stopped to show kindness to children, the blind, the lame, the demon possessed, even a widow whose only son had died. Help me emulate His example so I can help build His kingdom. Show me ways I can make an impact to the hurting travelers around me. Remind me of the pain others carry along this road we all trod. Use me completely.

I ask this in the precious name of the One who showed kindness to all, Jesus Christ. Amen

1 CORINTHIANS 13:4

Love does not envy.

Dear Heavenly Father,

I come before Your perfect throne of grace in the filthy rags I own. My sin-filled heart is so embarrassing to expose. You see all there is. You know my weaknesses and imperfections, yet You love me anyway. That's why it's called grace. Thank You for loving me.

You give me the love I don't deserve because that's Your heart. Your love is so strong You can't keep it to Yourself. You made me so there'd be someone to love You in return. You came and gave me the only perfect sacrifice imaginable just so I can come before You now and for all eternity. Thank You for making me.

Your love letter to me tells me love doesn't desire what someone else has. This is so hard to implement in my daily life. My job begs me to compare myself to those doing the same work. My society measures success by numbers. Thank You for accepting me.

When I look at sales numbers, or number of followers, or any number of other indicators of greatness, I too often feel left behind in this race called life. Satan hurls his fiery dart at me that says, "Your efforts aren't as good as someone else, so just give this business up." Thank You for understanding me.

Give me the focus I need to press on with the calling You gave me. Help me feel Your presence when I strive for Your glory. Grow my work to reach the audience You have for it to impact. Give me a peace that my reach may not be as large as someone else's numbers, but that doesn't make it any less significant. Thank You for choosing me.

If the widow's two mites made Jesus stop and notice, then I can be assured You are pleased with everything I do. Even if the effort is never appreciated by another human, let me know You are pleased with it. Sometimes my offering is Your way of speaking to my heart. Console my heart with that thought. Let me keep striving for an audience of one. Thank You for desiring me.

I lay this offering at Your feet in the name of Jesus Christ. Amen

1 CORINTHIANS 13:4

Love does not boast.

Dear Heavenly Father,

I stand in awe as I come to Your throne. My knees hit the floor as I approach You in reverence. My face comes in contact with the tiles as I fall completely prostrate in Your presence. I trust You because I know Your love is immense and intense. I worship You amazed.

You gave Your Son for me, so why would You want anything but the best for me? The trials of this life will either cause me to take my eyes off You, or I'll cling to You even stronger. Help me choose the latter option. Be my anchor in the storm I face. I admit my dependence.

Keep my attitudes in check as I serve You in my daily life. Even though I'm a child of the King of kings, keep my feet firmly planted on the ground as I march according to Your orders. Don't allow my tongue to take control of my motives and attitudes. I confess my weakness.

Let people I serve in Your name know my motives are to further Your kingdom, not mine. Use my words to encourage others, not place my works above anyone else. When this tendency comes into play, correct me so I fall in line with Your plan for me and those around me. I plead Your correction.

Grant me the heartfelt desire to love everyone I come in contact with. For some, this will be the only contact they have with this emotion. Our world has so maligned feelings and twisted definitions that few know the true meaning of love. I desire Your compassion.

Use me to display Your love to the hurting masses. Let me be Your hands and feet as I reach out to others with little thought for myself. Remove any impure motives from me as I set out to love others. May they see Jesus when they look at me. I seek Jesus's humility.

I ask this in the name of Jesus, the name above every name. Amen

1 CORINTHIANS 13:4

Love is not proud.

Dear Heavenly Father,

I stand before You totally awestruck by Your gracious love for me. You gave me a way to reach You that I could never attain on my own efforts. Though Your gift is free to me, it cost You Your one and only Son. Let me never forget that.

When the time came to place all the sins of mankind on Him, You covered the face of the earth with absolute darkness. This was the cup Jesus agonized over in the Garden of Gethsemane. Let me never forget this ultimate price that was paid as You purchased my soul for eternity. Help me ever appreciate this.

The sin of pride is always reaching into my heart. I can always look at others and see some who are seemingly lower than me. Help me never look down at anyone, no matter how small, insignificant, or pathetic they appear to me. Let me always remember this.

Remind me that Jesus died for them too. When I see someone "lower" than me, break my heart so that I bend my knees and stoop down to their level in order to help them any way I can.

May I always remember that the ground at the foot of the cross is absolutely level. None of us can reach heaven on our own works. Help me somehow comprehend this.

When I look down at others, it takes my vision the opposite direction You long for it to be. Keep me looking up for Your direction for my life. Remind me that it's only a quick turn of events, and I too could be standing in that unemployment line, or collecting cans for a few bucks, or contemplating doing the unthinkable in order to make it in life. May I always understand this.

Keep me humble enough to look people in the eyes when I hear their side of the story. Use me to give them Your hope through Jesus. Give me the words and actions that will reach their hearts for You. Grant that I treat others as I'd want to be treated. Let me always desire this.

It's only by the ultimate sacrifice Jesus made for me that I can come to You now. Amen

1 CORINTHIANS 13:5

Love is not rude.

Dear Heavenly Father,

I come to You ashamed by my actions. I haven't behaved according to the standard You set by Your Son. Forgive me for my shortcomings. Your smile never fades as I come to You. Your embrace is as warm and inviting as ever. Keep me close to Your heart.

Your strong arms are as gentle as the first time I felt them. Thank You for loving me without condition. Thank You for Your promise to never leave me nor forsake me. I need that compassionate commitment more than ever. Keep me wrapped in Your love.

It's a constant struggle for me to keep others ahead of myself. Remind me not to barge in ahead of another's words. Help me hear what they have to say before I think about what I'm going to say next. Grant me the compassion to allow another to cut in front of me without being upset. Keep me mindful of my place.

They have an even harder time dealing with their sinful nature because they don't know Your Son on a personal level. Use my gracious attitude to speak to their heart so they desire to be like me as they see Your Son being lived out in my life. Keep me obedient to You.

I need Your Spirit's control to live this new life out. Give me a bigger dose of compassion for others to counter my own selfishness. Remind me of the acronym for joy: **J**esus, **O**thers, **Y**ou. Keep me prioritized properly.

Help me keep Jesus at the front of my thoughts then other's needs before my own. If that means setting my own work aside to help someone else, then give me a glad heart to do just that. Keep me hungry to help others.

It's only because of Jesus's love for me I can come to You. Amen

1 CORINTHIANS 13:5

Love is not self-seeking.

Dear Heavenly Father,

I come before You because of who You are, not because I deserve to be in Your presence. Your love has transformed me into a person who looks out for others interests and needs. I wouldn't have become this way on my own. Use me to change others.

Left to myself, I'd simply look out for my own needs and desires. Your love, shown to me by Jesus's death and resurrection, has left an indelible mark on my soul. I am now Your child because I accepted Your gift of grace. I am forever changed from inside by Him. Transform me to mold others.

I still have a tendency to meet my own wants first. Help me see how I can be used by You to bring comfort to other weary travelers on this road of life. As Paul reminds me in today's passage, help me seek others' needs ahead of my own. Remind me to see others.

Break my heart to reach out in love to those in need. Humble me to the point of not even thinking of my desires before I help someone else out. Use me to make a difference like Jesus did. May my hands hold hope, my arms give hugs, and my eyes speak love. Use me as Your vessel of love. Blind me to love others.

I'm told I need to build a platform to be successful. I need to stand out and get noticed. Keep me focused on others as I get noticed in whatever sphere of influence You have for me. Use me to reach out to others and help them along on their journeys. Build me to help others.

Don't allow me to draw attention to myself as much as I draw attention to Jesus. Let me be Your light in this dark world. Lights are always most prominent in the deepest darkness. Remind me that as I shine Your light, I'll attract attention in a positive way, not as something that brings attention to me. Shine me to direct others.

Use me in Jesus's name. Amen

1 CORINTHIANS 13:5

Love is not easily angered.

Dear Heavenly Father,

I kneel before You a broken person. My imperfections are all the more obvious in Your presence. I'm so grateful for the sacrifice of Jesus that bridges the chasm that would otherwise separate me from You. Welcome me into Your presence.

Thank You for choosing to see me as though You're looking at Jesus because I chose to accept His gift to me. As an emotional creature, I'm brought to tears by this amazing realization. Accept me as Your child.

My emotions are hard to control sometimes. Anger is one of the worst ones to tame. I so long to have things always work for me that I get upset when they don't. Forgive me for this selfish tendency. Reform me for Your service.

Help me see others as You choose to see me. Give me Your eyes of compassion as I look at those around me. Grant me the patience to forgive and the grace to forget wrongs done. Help me see as Jesus does, always looking at what people will become, not what they are now. Mold me into Your image.

Remind me there is a point at which I should become angry at what is occurring. Even Jesus showed this emotion at the Temple when He chased off the money changers. Yes, I can be angry without sinning. Embolden me for Your passion.

Help me achieve the balance of being angry at the appropriate time without sinning. Give me a spine that stands up to injustices I see. Build my courage to face evil head on. Don't let me back down when I take a stand for You. Flavor all I do with love. Use me as Your ambassador.

I plead this in Jesus's name. Amen

1 CORINTHIANS 13:5

Love keeps no record of wrongs.

Dear Heavenly Father,

Thank You for Your mercy. Thank You for Your grace. Thank You, most of all, for Your love. Only a perfect God would give Himself as the ultimate sacrifice so I can have a deep relationship with Him. I'm beholden to Your grace.

This is proof that Your love knows no limits. You will go to any length to bring me to You. Your perfect memory can never forget anything. You choose to not remember my sins just so I can commune with You. I'm amazed by Your choice.

My sin-filled mind has a much harder time choosing to forget wrongs done. I'm more likely to hold onto a hurt than to let it go. I somehow feel I have a right to cling to a pain because it isn't fair. I'm ashamed by my action.

Remind me this bitterness is an acid that's eating a hole in my soul. The person who caused the pain has likely moved on with their life. This acid is only hurting me. Move by Your Holy Spirit to help me release this pain into Your hands. I'm pleading in my agony.

The first step I need to take in this journey of forgetting wrongs is the step of forgiveness. Give me the grace to humble myself to the point of not holding onto this pain any longer. Please take it from me now. I'm asking on my knees.

Remind me of how much You've forgiven me so I can turn that around to forgive others. Help me remember the past cannot be changed so I should let it go. Yes, I feel my burden becoming lighter already. Now I can more easily run the race set before me. I'm ready for Your service.

Thank You for this gift first displayed by Jesus. Amen

1 CORINTHIANS 13:6

*Love does not delight in evil but
rejoices with the truth.*

Dear Heavenly Father,

I come into Your presence with the assurance of Your love for me. My trembling heart melts when I see You smile as I approach Your throne. Even so, Lord, I fall to my knees before You. I bow in submission.

How can the created one do anything less in the company of the One who created me? Thank You for reaching out to me in love by Jesus's atoning death and life-giving resurrection. This action has overcome Satan's hold on me. I love in return.

I still have this bent toward selfish urges in my life. My survival instinct takes root and spreads into all corners of my heart, like a potted plant that's been in the same holder too long. Choking roots are all that remain. I struggle for survival.

In desperation, many lash out at society in order to breathe. Thank You for showing me the fresh air of Jesus's love on me.

Grow me now into His likeness. May others see my fruit and ask what makes me different. I ask in submission.

Give me the courage to stand up and call evil what it is, even if society tries to change the definition. Use me to focus attention where it belongs. Use my light to shine the spotlight on Your truth. I respond in obedience.

Grant me the desire to tell Your truth to this dying world in need of Jesus's love and compassion. Use me to demonstrate Your heart in outstanding ways to reflect attention on the love given through Jesus. I surrender in servitude.

It's in His mighty name that I ask this now. Amen

1 CORINTHIANS 13:7

Love always protects.

Dear Heavenly Father,

    I come to You as a frightened little child. This world I live in is so scary. Evil lurks around every corner. Sometimes it feels like there's no safe place to hide from it. Thank You for accepting me.

    You promise me in Your Word that You'll never leave me, nor forsake me. This is why I cling to You now. Without You, I'd be as aimless as most of the people I meet. Give me Your warm embrace as I crawl upon Your lap for comfort. Thank You for holding me.

    Remind me that I too have a responsibility to protect the less fortunate in my society from the evil in this world. Grant me the wisdom and courage to stand up and place my very body in harm's way when necessary. Thank You for emboldening me.

    Help me help others who are doing just that in places of the world I can't be in. I lift them up to You now. Please give them some angelic assistance to overcome the forces of evil that they're encountering right now. Thank You for hearing me.

Open my eyes to any way I might be unknowingly perceived as someone to be protected from. You know I long to be on the side of good as I fight this fight of faith. Thank You for understanding me.

But sometimes, others see things very differently than I intend them to be. Lift the fog of doubt so all can see my heart's cry is to love in the name of Jesus. May my love be seen as Your love to those involved so everyone can know You better. Thank You for using me.

I ask these things in the name of Jesus, my Savior. Amen

1 CORINTHIANS 13:7

Love always trusts.

Dear Heavenly Father,

I pause as I come before You now. I wait for Jesus to wash the dirt off my feet. This world has a way of making me impure in imperceptible ways. Thank You for making a way for me to safely approach Your holy place without reproach. I come in reverence.

I bow as I come into Your majestic presence. Your smile is the most precious thing I live for. Grant me wisdom and perseverance as I share Your love message that You have entrusted to me. I request in submission.

Trust is such a difficult virtue to live out. I know how many times I couldn't be trusted. A confidence slips out in a conversation I'm having, and I so long to unsay what's been said. But it's too late. I admit in shame.

Thank You for friends who can be trusted. Help me as I strive to be a more trustworthy person. Allow my love to overcome any barriers I have so I can give trust to those closest to me. I strive to improve.

Give me a heart of compassion to forgive those who have broken a trust with me. Let Your love show through me as I reach out in love so Your heart is on display. Use me as Your instrument of love to heal broken hearts as Jesus so earnestly did. I implore in obedience.

Thank You for showing me the importance of this virtue in my efforts to love. Grant me the ability to release my selfish tendency to take control. Help me trust those I love. I ask in humility.

I pray this in the awesome name of Jesus Christ. Amen

1 CORINTHIANS 13:7

Love always hopes.

Dear Heavenly Father,

I come to You with aching hands. The world says I'm supposed to tie a knot when I feel I'm at the end of my rope and hang on. My strength is failing as I try this under my own power. Where else can I turn?

You simply stretch out Your hands and say, "Trust Me." The calm assurance in Your voice gives me the one thing I've been missing in my struggle: hope. A glimpse at Your smile gives me the confidence to take the challenge. I let go of my rope.

During the time of free fall, doubts surface in my mind. Did I think this all the way through? Was there no other way? I recall Your words: "Trust Me." You are my only hope. Who else loves me so?

I land on Your strong hands and breathe a sigh of relief. The surprising gentleness of such powerful hands catches me off guard. Why did I ever doubt You? I open my eyes and see Your warm smile again. When I roll over to stand, I see my very name written on Your palm. Why have I never seen this?

"You've been Mine all along." My breath is again knocked out of my lungs. Then I realize, I've been here all the time. Your mighty hand closes around me in a soothing embrace. When did this all begin?

"I will never let you go." Not only is my hope restored, but so is my vitality. Use me as You see fit to spread this message of hope to every hurting soul holding on to the end of their rope. Move by Your Spirit to all I reach and bring them into Your holy family forever. How can I do less?

I pray this in the name of the only one worthy, Jesus Christ. Amen

1 CORINTHIANS 13:7

Love always perseveres.

Dear Heavenly Father,

My tired body comes to you again in need of refreshment. You lift me on Your lap and give me a meal. I fall asleep in Your trusting arms after I eat. Thank You for treating me right. You are the best Father.

Your love is very evident to me. I awake renewed. You always come through for me when I come to You. A warm hug and a smile sends me on my way. This needed encouragement enables me to continue my assignment. You are my constant comfort.

Remind me this journey I'm on isn't a sprint but a marathon. Help me pace myself to stay the course for the long haul. You didn't call me to live in isolation. I come in contact with hurting people everyday. You are the source of hope.

Give me the fortitude to get the word out to each individual I connect with to further Your kingdom. It's not about me as much as it's about the mission You have me deliver. The message is the key. You are the reason to love.

There are days when I have so many balls I'm juggling that I want to stop the madness and call it quits. But Your mission that's planted inside me won't allow that. So, please, give me the stamina to keep putting one foot in front of the other as I trudge along this often lonely road. You are my source of strength.

One step at a time is often all I can do, but it's all You ask of me. Thank You for understanding my frailties and using me anyway. This good work You began in me must be completed. You are my only sustenance.

It's in the matchless name of Jesus I bring this petition before You. Amen

1 CORINTHIANS 13:8

Love never fails.

Dear Heavenly Father,

I come again to the foot of Your throne. With eager anticipation, I search Your eyes and await Your words for me. Your love for me is the main thing that keeps me going on the hard days I face. I'm so grateful You chose me as Your adopted child. Guide my life.

Continue to deepen this relationship as I grow stronger in my Christian walk. Thank You for speaking directly to me by giving me the Bible in my language. Thank You for the faith to trust You for those aspects of You that are too difficult for my finite mind to comprehend. Grant me wisdom.

This look I've made into the virtues that make up this emotion called love has been so enlightening. Help me by Your Holy Spirit to apply what I've learned and make it more a part of my life. Help me trust that You have me on an individual track that doesn't need me to compare myself to anybody else. Keep me humble.

Give me the patient perseverance to forgive the wrongs done to me just as Jesus was able to ask forgiveness for those murdering His innocent life. Grant me kind eyes that look past my own interests and into those hurting souls around me who need Your love too. Use me admirably.

Thank You for the promise that love never does fail. It's the only thing I'll bring to heaven with me when my time comes to enter into Your presence. The spiritual gifts You grant me will no longer be necessary. My faith will be revealed before me as I see You face-to-face. Propel me onward.

My hope will be realized as the warmth of Your love engulfs me by Your light that knows no shadows. The family unity I'll experience will be like nothing I can even comprehend now. I thank You for this future love that I'm only touching in my life now. Use me to spread the message of Your love to others who need it too. Focus my attention.

It's in the mighty name of Jesus I ask this. Amen

THE FRUIT OF THE SPIRIT

GALATIANS 5:22

Part of the fruit of the Spirit is love.

Dear Heavenly Father,

I come to You a bit shaken today. This world's cruelty has done a number on me again. Jesus was absolutely right when He said I'd have trouble in this world. Please hold me tightly again. Thank You for not hesitating to do that. Fold me in Your arms.

I feel Your mercies being renewed in me like a morning sunrise. The warmth is penetrating my very soul. You are so much better that any earthly father I ever encountered. You're the best. Surround me in Your love.

I begin to partake of what's known as the fruit of the Spirit today. This fruit has many layers to it. Each delectable bite will bring me even closer to You in our relationship. Draw me into Your heart.

I just completed a journey perceiving the many facets of this first layer: love. If I could stop here, it seems as though that would be enough, but life is much more complicated than that. I require every bite of this fruit from You. It seems this first sweet bite would cover all the ingredients. Build me with Your wisdom.

My sinful nature won't allow me to express Your love as it should be done. Help me dive into each layer to become more like Jesus. Use me to inform others of Your ultimate love for all mankind. Remind me of my responsibility. Your sacrifice of becoming one of us and dying in our place is so incredible, yet so You. If I fail to tell others, it would be like a beggar finding an abandoned delivery truck full of food and refusing to let anybody else know about it. That's not love; that's greed. Break me for Your service.

Break through my stubborn heart to reach out in love to everybody I meet. Stretch me out of my comfort zone to become Jesus to the least of these, my brothers. Love is the attribute we all long for yet so few receive. Use me to show You.

Jesus even told me to reach out to my very enemies in love. I need the power of Your Holy Spirit to live that out. Help me break through the barriers I've erected as self-protection. Let me replicate Your hug for me as I hug those who truly need it too. Reflect You in my life.

It's in the glorious name of the ever-loving Jesus I pray. Amen

GALATIANS 5:22

Part of the fruit of the Spirit is joy.

Dear Heavenly Father,

I skip into the presence of my heavenly Abba whistling a tune. Your laughter shows me Your pleasure at my demeanor. You so long for me to live my saved life abundantly. I so want to dance.

Too often I let the weight of this world's pressure keep me from enjoying much. You desire to dance with me. Remind me to dance in Your sight. Give me such an overflow of joy I can't hold back, no matter who is watching. I really can't hold still.

My second bite into Your spiritual fruit gives me Your joy to share with those around me. Unlike happiness that is derived from outward circumstances, joy comes from within my very soul. I do want to reflect this.

The activity of Your Spirit inside me should be obvious to those I come in contact with. How did I lose this aspect of my relationship with You? Ignite a renewed joy in me that surprises my friends and family. I so want to stand out.

May everyone who sees me notice the joy that should have been bubbling up from me all along. Forgive me for quenching this part of the Holy Spirit's activity in my walk. I can't help but smile.

Let my smile be the catalyst that brings people to me to ask what's making me so happy in such a trying time as that in which I live. I am, after all, on the winning side of this spiritual battle, no matter what the situation looks like at this time. I'm glad we win.

Your Word tells me there's a time for mourning and weeping, but it also says there's a time for dancing and laughter. May Your joy so fill me that the times of joy outweigh the times of sadness. I do want to laugh.

Give me a fresh glimpse of my future so the times I live in can be endured with a lighter pack on my back. Let the joy set before me lead me on to Your upward calling in Christ Jesus. I'm adopted as Yours.

It's in the name of Jesus, who overcame sin's penalty, I pray. Amen

GALATIANS 5:22

Part of the fruit of the Spirit is peace.

Dear Heavenly Father,

I come to You today with a jumble of emotions. The news is filled with stories of wars and natural disasters all around the world. My own home is tense with strife and derision. Where else can I turn?

I'm told to take a day each year to think about what I'm thankful for. It's so easy to get caught up in the negativity that I lose my clear focus of what You consider important. You lift me on Your lap and give me that warm hug and smile. I now relax. Who else can comfort?

The next bite of Your Spirit's fruit brings me peace. Your Word promises me a peace that passes understanding. I've tasted of that unexplainable peace. I think it's a foreshadowing of what awaits me when I finally come into Your presence. How else can I explain it?

Your perfect holiness holds no stress. With You, all is well. You have everything under Your sovereign control. I need constant reminders of that in this seemingly out-of-control world I live in. What else can satisfy?

This battlefield I live in holds very little in the way of peace. Governmental peace treaties are too quickly broken when one side sees an advantage they can take in the interim. My heart is broken when a promise is not kept by a loved one. Who else can help?

This shouldn't surprise me when I consider there are opposing forces seriously engaged in winning this war for every soul they can get. Remind me the outcome is not in doubt. Why else would this go on?

In the end, Your kingdom will come. Things will be done according to Your plan. Help me hold strongly to that anchor when the storm tempests pull me away from You. What else can I cling to?

Let others see Your peace in me so they ask me about You. Thank You for coming to us and being the sacrifice we need to cross over to Your presence. Give me the peace that Jesus showed as He stood in front of Pilate. Remind me I don't need to understand this peace to enjoy it. How else can I continue?

It's in the magnificent name of Jesus, the Prince of peace, I come to You now. Amen

GALATIANS 5:22

Part of the fruit of the Spirit is patience.

Dear Heavenly Father,

I rush into Your throne room today harried by all the seasonal hustle and bustle. My mind is on the next thing on my to-do list. I want to get past this time with You quickly so I can go on to my other obligations. Please speed this up.

You wait for me to draw close enough to You to take my hand. You gently pull me in and slowly lift me on Your lap. I squirm. You pull me close with Your warm hug. A surprising serenity surrounds me. I let out a deep sigh and relax. Please keep this up.

My next bite into the fruit of the Spirit promises me patience. This virtue is becoming harder to find and more difficult to maintain. Computers have sped up my already fast-paced life into a cyber-speed whirlwind. Please help me cope.

I know what I want, and I want it now, if not sooner. You whisper in my ear, "My timetable is eternal, my child." A warmth fills my face as I blush in embarrassment. I'm so caught up in my own little world I forget Your mission. Your kingdom must be filled. Please keep reminding me.

Train me to put the important things ahead of the urgent ones. Rearrange my perspective to match Yours. Ground me with the promise that You are sovereign. Nothing is out of Your control. Please maintain Your control.

Pry my fingers off the stuff I've accumulated here. Focus my thoughts on the only things I can bring to heaven with me: my own soul and those You want me to reach for Your kingdom. Use my words—both spoken and written—to touch hearts with Your love and truth. Please take my stuff.

This writing journey You have me on is ripe with lessons on patience. Let me learn from each one. Help me release control of my stories and make the changes that will enhance my books into something that will be a fragrant offering to You. Please give me wisdom.

Give me a calm trust that You are working behind the scenes at publishing houses to excite the best company to bring my books to print in Your time. Give me the fortitude to build my platform into something that will bring Your stories out to as many people as possible when the time for promoting my books comes. Remind me this is a marathon, not a sprint. Please grant me determination.

It's only in the power of the mighty name of Jesus I come to You. Amen

GALATIANS 5:22

Part of the fruit of the Spirit is kindness.

Dear Heavenly Father,

I knock gently on Your throne room door. I hear a light chuckle as You say, "Come in, My child." Your smile draws me close to You once again. I bow to my knees at Your feet. You have my reverence.

As I stand, You hold Your hands toward me. I step close enough for You to lift me on Your lap. That familiar warm embrace engulfs me. I melt at the thought that I don't deserve any of this. Your kindness is unbelievable. You hold my devotion.

My next bite into the fruit of the Spirit brings me kindness. This ingredient means much more than mere politeness. Treating others in kind is a better definition. You have my attention.

As Jesus described it, "Do unto others as you would have them do unto you." My selfish nature so prickles at this thought. I'd rather have my own way in matters. I do need the help of the Holy Spirit to live out this trait of Your children. You need my desire.

Part of my problem is I tend to think I deserve to be treated better than I'm treated. Help me put myself last in any equation when I think about how I'll respond to others' shortcomings. You want my will.

Help me see others as Jesus sees them: adrift on an open sea with no anchor to hold them firm. Use me as the catalyst that draws them to Your hope and foundation. May Your kindness be on display in me every day. You desire my life.

Give me actions that show Your kindness in action. Use my words to give people the insight as to what makes Christians unique. Break their hearts and wills when they come in contact with me. You have my life.

Guide them by Your Holy Spirit into Your kingdom. This is how I so long to be used by You. Help me increase the number of people who will spend eternity with You. Please increase Your kingdom with me.

It's in the mighty, matchless name of Jesus Christ I come to You now. Amen

GALATIANS 5:22

Part of the fruit of the Spirit is goodness.

Dear Heavenly Father,

I come to you today with one hand stretched forward as I look behind me. One year is ending; its regrets will dog me for a long time without Your help. The pain is so fresh in my heart. Rescue me again.

The promise of a fresh start in the coming year is a frightening hope I try to cling to. I don't have a great track record of making the most of these opportunities to be a better person. You lift me on Your lap and embrace me to get my attention. I look into smiling eyes. Hold me close. Of course You know my weaknesses. You're the One who made me the person I am. You have a plan to work things together for good, even the "mistakes" I make. Remind me anew.

Romans 8:28 promises me all things will work together for good; verse 29 explains that the good You are working in me is to make me more like Your Son Jesus Christ. Please help me focus on

Your definition of good. The world's definition is so far off Your mark. Establish me aright.

Remind me I'm engaged in a battle on this planet. A spiritual war wages all around me even though I can't always see it with my natural eyes. It rears its ugly head when I turn on the news and hear of yet another mass shooting. Focus me properly.

Satan has gotten hold of another weary traveler and declared his brand of "good." Use me to reach out to as many people as possible in as many ways imaginable as many times as are made available to me with Your good news. Use me boldly.

Strengthen me with Your power to boldly go where I never dreamed I could go as You lead me on. Grant me the courage to take risks for You. Stretch me to become more than I ever thought I could be to further Your kingdom's agenda. Grow me exponentially.

You are light. You are love. You are good. Use me to give these truths to those around me. Even when they don't believe me, let me proclaim Your truth anyway. I am Your child. Make me good too. Change me, Father.

It's only because of Jesus's awesome rescue He did for me on the cross I can come before You. Amen

GALATIANS 5:22

Part of the fruit of the Spirit is faithfulness.

Dear Heavenly Father,

As I approach the door to Your throne room of grace, the hinges swing the obstacle out of my way voluntarily. Your smile invites me to come to You. I can't help but smile. You are so steady.

I'm so grateful You enjoy my company even though my mind can't understand it. Why are You always there for me? Your faithfulness is such a core of Your being that it amazes me. Let me soak in Your grace and love as often as I can. You are always there.

Thank You for offering a measure of faithfulness to me as Your child. I so long for a better practice of this attribute of You. Help me be more reliable and sure. You are so gracious.

Use me to attract others to You by my humble spirit that is there when people need me. Give me the wisdom to know when to set my agenda aside to aid another soul who is struggling. Give me eyes that see the need in someone's face. You are so bountiful.

Remind me this world is not my home. Guide me as to how to tell others they can have that hope too. Keep me steadfast in Your plan for reaching the lost. You are so welcoming.

Grant me the courage to remain strong in my resolutions to be an ambassador of Your kingdom. Give me a life that resembles Jesus more and more each day. That is my deepest heart's desire. Let others see that growth in me. You are so empowering.

Obstacles will come to divert me from Your calling for my life. Help me remain pure in my motives and sure in my source of strength. I can do nothing without Your power to move me along. You are so strong.

Give me Your words as I live for Your glory and kingdom. Keep me anchored on Your Word for my message. Use me to bring others to You in my life before my words are even spoken. You are so faithful.

It's in the mighty name of Jesus Christ I stand in Your presence. Amen

GALATIANS 5:23

Part of the fruit of the Spirit is gentleness.

Dear Heavenly Father,

I come to You today smudged with dirt. My hair is out of place. My shirt is missing a button. My sleeve is torn. This world has really beaten me down. It's a maddening crush of people I live in. I need Your acceptance.

Your smile draws me forward. You gently lift me on Your lap and wrap me in Your loving embrace. The sudden warmth calms me to my core. Thank You for understanding and loving me no matter what. I love Your embrace.

My nature begs me to fight back. Retaliation seems the best course of action. It's what I'm told to do by the society I live in. But You give me a spirit of gentleness to draw people to You who don't understand Your ways. I desire Your strength.

As Your ambassador, it's up to me to stand out because I'm Your child. I'm to be different because You are different. They need to see this difference to know there is something better for them. I want Your compassion.

Gentleness and meekness are seen as weaknesses today. In fact, it takes a lot of strength to exhibit these traits. Jesus stood out in His day by living these out. I follow His example.

Thank You for promising to give me the courage to live this out in my day too. Remind me I'm not living to please the people I need to reach; I need to please You, Heavenly Father. Grant me wisdom to carry this walk out properly. I need Your vision.

The path I trod is full of distractions and false ways. Help me avoid the dead ends that want to trap me where I don't belong. Guide me in Your way by Your light. I thirst Your refreshment.

Slake my thirst by drawing me to Your Word on a regular basis. As my mind fills with Your truth, the falsehoods I hear will be pushed out. Keep me gentle as I present Your gospel to this dying generation You've placed me in. I hunger for Your nourishment.

It's only because of the power of Jesus's name I come to you. Amen

GALATIANS 5:23

Part of the fruit of the Spirit is self-control.

Dear Heavenly Father,

I crack the throne room door open and peek inside. As I push the door open farther, I see You waiting for me. You motion for me to come in. Your warm smile and outstretched hands invite me in. Your love is quite intense.

I step back and look myself over before I come to You. My gaze is on the floor as I walk closer to You. When I see the throne, I look up. You pull me on Your lap, again. Your grace is truly amazing.

My final bite into the fruit of the Spirit promises me self-control. To be frank with You, I feel like I just bit the pit inside this fruit. You must know how much I need help in this area. Your discipline is exact.

If I have a handle on my eating and exercise, I know I could use better judgment on how I spend my time. There's always something I should do better. Why did You save the last bite as the one I feel the most responsible for? Your wisdom still astounds me.

A close examination of Your Word shows me that when I delight myself in You, You give me the desires of my heart. I so long to be a vessel that can be useful in building Your kingdom. Your mercy is ever faithful.

I also know You promise me wisdom if I ask You for it. As I partake of this spiritual fruit, I realize it's becoming a part of me with each bite. This means You will help me conquer the demons of self-doubt to become a victor. Your encouragement is always there.

Thank You for aiding me along this difficult road of my earthly life. Thank You for encouraging me to continue to improve. Thank You for accepting me as I am and using me anyway. Your compassion never fails.

Help me become more like Jesus every day so people can more easily see Him in me and come to me to ask what makes me so different. Thank You for adopting me into Your spiritual family and making me one of Your own. Your choosing is very sure.

It's only because of Jesus's self-sacrifice I can come to You now. Amen

GALATIANS 5:22-23

But the fruit of the Spirit is love, joy, peace, patience, kindness, goodness, faithfulness, gentleness, and self-control. Against such things there is no law.

Dear Heavenly Father,

I come to you filled now. There's a skip in my step as I approach Your throne of grace. I have consumed Your fruit and found it very good. My walk is lighter. My smile matches Yours. You throw a little tickle in Your hug for me. Thank You for being such a fabulous Daddy. I couldn't ask for any better.

Thank You for putting all of these aspects of You into a single piece of fruit for me. It's so like You to give me the whole package at once. You don't want me picking and choosing which qualities I think I need or want. Grant me the fortitude to put these attributes to use as Jesus did in His life on this earth.

Help me love as Jesus loved, unconditionally. Don't let my pride or prejudices get in the way of me showing Your love to everyone I meet.

Give me the joy Jesus exhibited, enthusiastically. I always picture Him laughing from the belly when He played with the children, no matter what others thought of Him.

Let me promote the peace of Jesus, unapologetically. Allow me to sleep while the storm is so severe around me others are panicked.

Grant me the patience of Jesus, forever. May I trust that You have everything under control, even when it appears everything is in chaos.

Allow me to show the kindness of Jesus, generously. Let me drop my guard as I reach out in love so people see the genuineness of my actions.

May I live out the goodness of Jesus, authentically. Make my motives so pure I'm embarrassed when others applaud my efforts to make a difference in this world.

Ground me in the faithfulness of Jesus, wholeheartedly. Fix my gaze on heaven while I see the needs on the earth with Your kingdom in mind.

Gift me with the gentleness of Jesus, continuously. Let me see the sinner caught up in the sin before I see the sin itself so I can reach out in love and acceptance of the person.

Build in me the self- control Jesus exhibited, purposefully. Help me drink the cup You place before me in Your time as it benefits Your kingdom, not mine.

Father, I need Your Spirit's strength to carry out this magnificent calling from You. Your Son left His indelible mark on this world. Use me to carry on His mission as I finish the race set before me.

It's in the mighty, matchless name of Jesus I pray. Amen

THE TEN COMMANDMENTS

EXODUS 20:2-3

I am the LORD your God who brought
you out of Egypt, out of the land of slavery.
You shall have no other gods before Me.

Dear Heavenly Father,

As I climb the mountain next to Moses, I feel Your presence in the dense cloud. Your glory would so overpower me You must be cloaked in something my eyes can't penetrate. Prepare me for the law You designed for me to live by. Remind me these laws are imposed to protect me, not to take my happiness away. My wrists and ankles are still raw from the chafing of the shackles of my slavery. For me, there's no turning back.

I no longer want the limits of the old life I once lived. I long to be impressed by Your love. As I enjoy the warmth of Your arms around me, help me embrace the plans You lay before me. Your plans are not to harm me but to give me hope for my future. I feel the refreshment to my soul already. Your light draws me forward to my eternal destiny. The road before me leads me on.

As I concentrate on You, I wonder how I could ever want any other god beside You. This world is so full of distractions. My eyes and heart are enticed to drift from Your presence constantly. Keep my focus on You. Sometimes that will feel painful to me, but do it to remind me of Your love. You need to remain my supreme love and desire. Keep my vision on the narrow road before me.

You have ways of getting my attention when I go overboard with my love for anything that takes Your place as number one in my life. The illness, or death, of one close to me can be such a thing. My life is so hard to keep in proper balance. Keep me humble, workable clay on Your potter's wheel. Mold me into a loving servant You can use mightily for Your kingdom. Give me mercy to carry my load.

It's only because of the awesome sacrifice of Jesus Christ I come before You now. Amen

EXODUS 20:4-5

You shall not make for yourself an idol in the form of anything in heaven above or on the earth beneath or in the waters below. You shall not bow down to them or worship them; for I, the LORD your God, am a jealous God.

Dear Heavenly Father,

The ground beneath my feet is still rumbling from the sound of Your voice. If I wasn't so convinced of Your love for me, I'd probably die in my tracks. May my reverence for You never cease. Remind me how You created all I see with mere spoken words. Continue to strike me with sheer awe whenever I contemplate Your power. Thank You for adopting me as Your child.

It's still such a foreign concept for my depraved nature to worship a spiritual being. My life is so wrapped up in what I see. Images surround me and scream for my attention every day. Remind me that it's Your energy I need in order to sustain my very existence. As Your child, I must derive my very sustenance from Your Word. Thank You for giving me Your strength.

Bring to mind everything I have set up that detracts my attention from You. Give me a proper focus as I examine my life. Grant me blunt honesty as I delve into my daily habits to discover what idols I've established. Strengthen me as I attempt to break free from their pull on my life and desires. Thank You for wanting my undivided devotion.

Give me a sincerity of motive here. Don't let this be mere lip service again. I'm so prone to postpone what I need to do for You. Show me what priorities I need to change to make me more like Jesus. I ask for wisdom and determination to make necessary changes. Help me see the enemy's attempts to thwart my resolve to remove those things that detract from my worship of You. Thank You for Your righteous jealousy.

I come before You by the only name that's worthy, Jesus Christ. Amen

EXODUS 20:7

You shall not misuse the name of the LORD your God, for the LORD will not hold anyone guiltless who misuses His name.

Dear Heavenly Father,

    I call You Father in the most reverent tone. You not only gave me my physical life, but You also adopted me into Your spiritual family and gave me my forever spiritual life, too. I so look forward to spending my eternal destiny with You so I can finally see You with my glorified eyes. Until that day, my faith leads me on to devote my very self to You and Your kingdom. Thank You for loving me so immensely.

    Since I don't have anything physical to point people to that will show them who You are, Your name is the best handle I have. This is why I need to give Your name so much respect. If the lost people I'm trying to reach see me mistreating Your name, they'll be put off faster than anything else. Renew in me the importance of reverencing Your name in all I do. Thank You for giving me such a standard.

You've given me stories to show how a relationship with You works out in this world. Guide my words to correctly declare Your attributes and attitudes to the very creatures You made out of nothing. If I stray from Your truth, give me loving people who'll show me the error of my way so I can correct it before my books see the printed page. Thank You for giving me this stewardship.

Keep my attitude pure as I write and speak. It's too easy to get caught up in the lure of shifting my focus on primarily making money with words. It's great when what I put out there brings in an income, but don't let that be my principal motive. Remind me that You are the audience I need to write for. I trust You to meet my needs out of Your abundance. Thank You for looking out for me.

It's out of the utmost reverence of the name above every name, Jesus Christ, that I pray now. Amen

EXODUS 20:8

Remember the Sabbath day by keeping it holy.

Dear Heavenly Father,

You who made all I see out of nothing but Your words. You didn't lose one ounce of energy in the entire process of creation, yet You set aside the seventh day to rest from Your labors. Since Your rest wasn't taken out of necessity, I can deduce it was made as an example for me to follow. Grant me wisdom in implementing this practice in my life. I do need time to recharge my body.

This world is so full of noise and distractions. My attention is continuously being called for in too many directions. Technology has made this need to unplug an even bigger challenge, and necessity, than ever before. Steel my resolve to take time away from the demands on me to slow down and listen to You. I need to purposefully come apart from my everyday life before I simply come apart. I do need time to recharge my soul.

Your Word is what I need to fill my thoughts with. Help me set aside quiet time to read, meditate, implement, and absorb the Bible on a personal level. Listening to sermons has its place, but it's not enough for me to really grow on. To meet You on a personal level, I need one-on-one time with You. Give me a determination to spend quality time in Your love letter to me. I do need time to recharge my mind.

You promise me a peace that passes my finite understanding. You can't give me that peace in a void. The more I abide in Your teachings, the more frequently I'll feel Your peace. I thank You for water in its many forms to relax me. A gurgling brook has a way of soothing me; the ripples on a small lake can mesmerize my mind; the crashing waves of a large body can bring awe. I do need time to recharge my spirit.

Thank You for coming down as one of us to give me a living example, Jesus Christ. Amen

EXODUS 20:12

Honor your father and mother, so that you may live long in the land the Lord your God is giving you.

Dear Heavenly Father,

I look to You as the epitome of the best example of a father. Jesus drove this point home so frequently while He walked among us. He pointed out that our earthly fathers may not always treat us with our best intentions in mind, but You always do. Even the bad things that happen to me serve a greater purpose for me in Your economy. In the end, they make me more like Jesus. Continue to mold me into His image.

Some of us didn't have our biological parents around for us to show honor to. Perhaps there was a father or mother who abandoned the family for their own selfish reasons. Help us work through the sting of that rejection we feel. They didn't mean to harm us emotionally that way. They simply ignored the debris of the fallout of their actions. Their own happiness took precedence over anything else. Help me move on to my future.

For those of us who did have both parents around for our entire growing up lives, there may still be some animosity to deal with. We would have thrived with more one-on-one time with either parent. We'll always wonder how we would have developed with that attention. Help us let go of the past and live lives that don't reproduce this activity when, or if, the time comes for us to be parents. Allow me to take ownership of my life.

The family unit is so important to You that You gave a promise to those who choose to abide by this law. The erosion of the family structure is collapsing at a staggering rate these days. Grant me the fortitude to keep at my assigned duty for You with all I have as long as I can. How I treat my parents is still a test of my relationship with You. Give me wisdom as I deal with issues in my life. May I honor You by honoring my parents.

I come to You, Father, by the one and only Son, Jesus. Amen

EXODUS 20:13

You shall not murder.

Dear Heavenly Father,

The somber tone of today's theme gives me pause. Could I actually kill another person? Am I actually capable of such an atrocity? If someone broke into my home, would it be considered murder, or self-defense? On the surface, I thought this was a mute point. Now, I'm not so sure. There's still a dark, sinful nature lurking inside me. Give me Your eyes to see the truth.

Of course there's more than one way to murder. Physical death is the most obvious thing I think of. But what about killing someone's reputation with my words? That sharp dagger of a muscle in my mouth is very capable of ruining another's character in a sentence. Since it dips its poison from my heart, help me do a heart check to measure my motives. Give me a heart that feels for others.

While I have my heart open, help me gauge my motives when I critique others' writing. It's too easy to want to try to dissuade someone who hasn't been writing as long as I have, but I see they're much closer to getting published than I am. Help me put my jealousy aside and help them in any way I can. Guide me on the path You have me on. Give me motives that celebrate with others.

There are certain people groups out there that I simply don't trust. I've heard they'd like to see me dead because I don't follow their beliefs. It's hard for me to not want harm for them. Jesus gave me an example for how to deal with this type of person. Help me point out the error of their way while still loving them. Give me a pure heart that looks past other's motives.

I pray this in the name that can transform even the hardest heart, Jesus Christ. Amen

EXODUS 20:14

You shall not commit adultery.

Dear Heavenly Father,

I come to you as a fallen creature. The dirt of this world is clinging to me as a fine dust that won't wash off. I do my best, but it comes back too quickly as I walk away from the shower. Of course, You already know this. That's why You came down as one of us to give Your life as my sacrificial death. You knew I'd never be able to reach You, so You came to me so humbly. Help me never forget Your love.

As a physical being, I'm attracted to the physical world around me. The desire for procreation You built within me has some pitfalls that come with it. There's an attraction to the opposite sex that must be curtailed many times for me to continue to honor You with my body. My society is telling me sex is okay in any consenting fashion. I know they aren't reading Your book. Keep me grounded in Your Word.

The enemy knows my weakness. He'll try anything and everything to get me to stumble in this battle. Help me guard my body by guarding my heart and mind. My eyes are the main entry point of these sinful lusts. For men, it's mainly the images and people we see that pull us into this mire. For women, it's more of an emotional attachment brought on by reading or building an innocent relationship. Shield me with a dogged determination.

You told me this sin is especially hurtful to You because it involves my body. My body is the temple You choose to abide in to help me walk this slippery slope of life. Remind me about the selfishness of my actions when I wallow in this arena. Help me flee as quickly as I can to Your safety. Grant me a renewed commitment to honor You by honoring my sexual duties. Reward me for my human sacrifice.

It's in the power found only in the name of Jesus Christ I come before You now. Amen

EXODUS 20:15

You shall not steal.

Dear Heavenly Father,

Your laws seem so commonsense to me, but there are those who don't follow Your standards who need straight talk from You. My society has established new guidelines for me to follow. Then they wonder why they're so dissatisfied with life. Guide me with Your wisdom and plan for me to follow. Keep my feet on the straight and narrow path that leads me to You. Keep me grounded.

Taking what isn't mine is something I was taught is bad when I was quite young. A blurring of that line has occurred as I got older. It isn't always physical things that I take. In search of my own personal happiness, I occasionally use people to my advantage. I play with emotions and desires to have them perform for me so I get something I shouldn't take. Keep me observant.

Forgive me for using people like I do. Remind me they're just as in need of a Savior as I am. They'll see Jesus in me when I treat them with respect and dignity just like Jesus always did. Use Your Holy Spirit to transform me into His likeness to the point that

I stand out. People will be drawn to me as I display Your love to them. Use me in this way. Keep me open.

Continue to guide my writing so I come up with fresh ideas and characters. Don't let me get lazy by taking from others. Direct my heart and mind as I choose to be used by You to reach people with words. Give me Your words to heal and refresh. Grant me wisdom and discernment in everything I write, even my e-mails. Keep me honest.

It's in the mighty name of Jesus Christ I come before You. Amen

EXODUS 20:16

You shall not give false testimony
against your neighbor.

Dear Heavenly Father,

I come to You in need of an answer. Who is my neighbor? You answered this as Jesus by telling me it's anybody I come in contact with at any time. The Internet has made my world incredibly small. As the Good Samaritan reached across racial lines to aid someone who was hurting, use me to lift others up, especially when I feel like setting them in their place. Keep me grounded in Your teachings.

Grant me patience, Lord. Help me think through the repercussions before I hit "send" on an e-mail or blog post. If it's not going to bring You glory, then guide me to hit "delete" instead. My depraved mind can too easily come up with justifications for my actions. Even when it's clear they have it coming to them, help me take the high road in everything I do. Keep me holy in my actions.

Honesty is the policy I so long to carry out. That line has become so blurred these days. Give me clarity in my thinking and truthfulness in my heart. Don't let me twist what I know is right to fit my agenda. Replace my heart with one like Jesus's heart. May my heart reach out in love at all times while having a boldness to confront evil and hypocrisy when I encounter it. Keep me focused on Your Kingdom.

Give me confidence in Your calling for me. Help me look past a bad review of something I wrote. If I'm representing You properly, I'm going to step on some toes. Remind me it isn't me they're raving against but You. Let me pray for those who so desperately need You. Use Your Spirit to convict them of their sinfulness. Bring them into Your family through my words. Keep me steadfast as Your ambassador.

It's in the power of the matchless name of Jesus I pray. Amen

EXODUS 20:17

You shall not covet your neighbor's house.
You shall not covet your neighbor's wife, or his
manservant or maidservant, his ox or his donkey,
or anything that belongs to your neighbor.

Dear Heavenly Father,

My arms are sore, and my eyes are tired as I come to You today. I've spent too much time reaching for things that belong to someone else. I stare through my neighbor's window far too long. Help me overcome this tendency to want what isn't mine to begin with. My depraved mind is too quick to think others have it better than me. Remind me they're likely doing the same thing to me. Give me a right perspective.

There's no good reason for me to be discontent with the things You've given me. You've placed me where You want me and given me the tools to get the job done. Let me focus on the task You've given me, not on what You've given someone else. Keep my motives pure and my thoughts right as I live my life for You. Thank You for allowing me the privilege of being Your servant here on earth. Ground me with right desires.

Your Word promises me that You make me lie down in green pastures. So why am I so anorexic while I drool over the grass in other fields? Let me taste and see that what You've provided for me is more than sufficient for me. Give me a hunger for Your purpose for my life. Keep me focused on being me, not on wanting to be someone else. Grant me a proper vision.

As the manna was provided each morning for Your people as they left slavery, keep me content on what You've provided me. You'll give me what I need to finish each day on Your schedule. Tomorrow will come with its own problems and demands. You are already in my tomorrow. Your provision will be there for me when I need it. Remind me of Your constant care.

I acknowledge it's only because of Jesus's ultimate sacrifice I come before You now. Amen

THE I AM STATEMENTS OF JESUS

JOHN 6:35

Then Jesus declared, "I am the bread of life.
He who comes to Me will never go hungry,
and he who believes in Me will never be thirsty."

Dear Heavenly Father,

I come to You with an ache I can't quite place. There's a satisfaction that's unmet. It's something I'm too familiar with. It always keeps me company even in the wee hours of the night. I ignore it for a time, but it comes back. I hide it in activity and "pleasures," but it's still there. It's an echo from Eden that haunts every human heart. Please, show me what starves me.

It's times like now that stem this pain. In Your presence I feel safe and loved. As I speak to You, I sense a belonging. A familial twinge is excited. A comfort is filling my heart and soul. My pulse slows as my blood pressure drops. A peace…yes, a peace is filling me now. I pull back from this unfamiliar territory. Dare I carry on? Please, assure me of Your love.

As Jesus, You stated to be the bread of life. Life…is that what I've been missing? Have I been feeding my soul empty calories all this time? Train me to feed on Your sustenance. As You supplied the Hebrews a daily need of manna in the wilderness, give me my daily bread too. Fill me with Your nourishment. Give me an abundance of You. Please, provide me with Your meals.

When I witness a sunrise, I'm reminded of Your renewed mercies. Help me to forgive myself as You forgive me. Let me let go of the past so I can concentrate on moving forward. Lock my hands on the plow You give me to use. Give me strength to endure the steps that falter beneath me. Nourish my soul as only You can, abundantly and whole. Please, focus my eyes on Your kingdom.

A commitment is what You require of me. An adoption is what You offer. The price was paid on the cross. Jesus died my death so I can live His life. His resurrection is proof of His overpowering love for me. He conquered my ultimate enemy, death, once and for all. Eternity with You as my Father is my potential destiny. Let me accept this gift now. Please, take me into Your family.

It's in the mighty name of the mighty warrior, Jesus Christ, I pray. Amen

JOHN 8:12

> When Jesus spoke again to the people
> He said, "I am the light of the world.
> Whoever follows Me will never walk in
> darkness, but will have the light of life."

Dear Heavenly Father,

I shield my eyes as I come into Your presence. My world is so dark. You are so full of light. The contrast is so awesome. None can compare to You. I'm so used to the darkness I grew up in that I still wallow in its familiarity. There's still a bit of pleasure in sin. Keep drawing me to Your light. Remind me of the consequences of wrong actions. Focus my desires on Your light.

As I'm called to carry Your light in this dimly lit planet You created help me see others who need to know of Your light. Use me as an ambassador to inform those groping around me of the source of light that will truly guide their steps to peace. Give me a new boldness to take Your light out of hiding and show everybody Your truth and life. Keep my attention on others.

Remind me of the necessity to be set apart for You. I don't have any reason to be dabbling in sin. Help me choose to remain in Your light so I'll continue to be a clean vessel that honors You with my life. You've sanctified me for Your glory. You set me apart to be different just because You delighted to do so. Help me remember that I am not my own but Yours. Delight my heart in Your glory.

Temptations and tests abound for me, even as Your child. Some days I must take it one step at a time. Other days I must flee as fast as I can. Give me the wisdom to know when I must do each in turn. Give me the fortitude to continue on the road You've chosen for me. It's not about me and my happiness but You and Your kingdom. Train my heart on You.

It's all because of Jesus that I come before You now. Amen

JOHN 10:7, 9

Therefore Jesus said again,
"I tell you the truth, I am the gate for the sheep."
"I am the gate; whoever enters through
Me will be kept safe."

Dear Heavenly Father,

Here I stand, nestled in with other followers of Christ. There's a comfort here…a belonging. Thank You for inviting me into Your fold. Your pen of protection means everything to me. On my own, I'm defenseless against the enemy and his forces. I need Your ever-protecting hand over me and around me. The assurance that You have overcome my greatest enemy gives me the hope I need to continue. Thank You for adopting me.

Knowing You will never leave me nor forsake me grounds me in a security of fortitude. I'm ready to face the obstacles life throws at me. Even on the hard days when I feel all alone, I know You're there with me. Remind me of this promise when my strength is low and my hope is dim. Grant me the faith to take the next step into the unknown for You and Your kingdom. Thank You for never leaving me.

In the first century, a shepherd would lie down in the opening of his pen to keep his sheep safe for the night. His sheep would know to stay in the security of that pasture because they trusted their shepherd. Predators would stay away from the sheep since they knew the shepherd would fight for his sheep with all of his might. Jesus couldn't have chosen a more apt illustration of His life. Thank You for protecting me.

As long as the shepherd blocked the opening, the sheep knew they needed to stay where they were. It was only when the shepherd gave the call to exit the pasture did the sheep venture out of their pen. Give me the trust to know when You've closed a door to me. Grow my patience to wait on Your timing to continue with my journey in the direction I feel You leading me. Thank You for controlling me.

I come to You now in the name of Jesus my Lord. Amen

JOHN 10:11, 14

I am the good shepherd. The good shepherd
lays down his life for his sheep.
I am the good shepherd; I know my
sheep and my sheep know me.

Dear Heavenly Father,

I follow close behind You with the other sheep. Your presence reassures me of my dependence on You. My inability to fend off predators or find proper sustenance is foremost on my mind. Left to my own devices, I'll stumble into messes I can't get myself out of. I need Your perspective and wisdom. I trust Your love and abilities. Keep me close to You.

I am such a stupid creature. You are the Creator of all things. Why would I venture away from Your protection of me? I wish I had the answer as I tend to do exactly that repeatedly. Do whatever You have to do to keep me in the green pasture You place me in. Keep me away from the rapids that try to pull me in while You lead me to quiet waters to quench my thirst. Keep me dependent on You.

Somebody hired by the shepherd to watch the sheep will bolt at the sign of trouble to protect himself. Only the best of shepherds has enough vested in the sheep to put his life on the line to protect his sheep to the point of death. Jesus proved to us what level of shepherd He is. His life meant nothing to Him. He gave it up willingly to bring me into His fold. Keep me reminded of Your sacrifice.

The enemy of all mankind gained only a short-term victory at Calvary. Jesus's love for me brought Him out of the grave to prove His power over my ultimate enemy— death. This plan that was made before man was made was carried out to give me access to the God of the universe on a personal level. Help me spread the news of this amazing gift that is offered to everyone. Keep me vigilant for You.

I come to You because of Jesus's sacrifice. Amen

JOHN 11:25-26

Jesus said to her, "I am the resurrection and the life. He who believes in Me will live, even though he dies: and whoever lives and believes in Me will never die."

Dear Heavenly Father,

I come before Your throne totally spent. My last ounce of energy was used to get here. I have nothing left. I've given my all and can't go on. From the prone position, I feel Your hand grasp my shoulder. A flow of energy courses my entire being. An upward lift guides me to my feet. The smile on Your face reminds me of why I need to come here now. Thank You for understanding my need.

I recall Your promise of life for those who believe Jesus is You in a human body. As long as I have breath in my lungs, I have a mission from You to carry out. With that call to action comes a source of strength to fulfill that task. Help me make Your agenda my agenda. This life is not about my happiness but Your kingdom. Thank You for giving me purpose.

When Jesus made this bold statement of His, there was a rotting corpse in a tomb. There was nothing Lazarus could do to change his situation. He was gone as far as anybody knew—until Jesus showed up and changed the whole scenario with His words. Jesus's words still give life to those who hear them. I take His words in by reading the Bible. Thank You for writing Your words.

As a writer, You've given me words to use to tell others of You and Your love. Give me Your words as I craft stories, poems, and prayers that honor You. Use me to bring hope and life to those who struggle for meaning in this life. Let me be the conduit that directs people to You. As much as I can, let me step in the shadows as I shine Your light in the darkness. Thank You for using me now.

It's in the matchless name of Jesus I pray. Amen

JOHN 14:6

Jesus answered, "I am the way and the truth and the life. No one comes to the Father except through Me."

Dear Heavenly Father,

I squint as I enter Your throne room. Your light is so pure and complete. My eyes are acclimated to the world I live in. I've grown accustomed to groping in the dark to find my way. My world offers so many versions of what they call truth. I'm too easily confused by these choices. The distractions draw me away from You and real truth. Keep me focused on You.

Jesus didn't waver when He declared to be *the way*. He knew there'd never be another who would come directly from You. Jesus is not one of many ways to Your presence. He is the one and only way. His blood was the blood foreshadowed by the Old Testament sacrifices. His death was the sacrifice to end all sacrifices. He showed me Your grace. Lead me directly to You.

Definitions these days are so fickle. Dictionaries aren't as reliable as they once were. Boundaries are always shifting like sand in the desert. Stability is unheard of in our culture. I live in a disposable society. Thank You for writing Your truth in a book and keeping it secure. Jesus is more than merely a good man with high moral teachings. He is *the truth*. Ground me solely in You.

There are so many enticements drawing me away from You. My world is endlessly tempting me to find "life" in various devices and deeds. Contentment and happiness are being confused with joy. The life Jesus offers is filled with joy and life abundantly. Temporary fixes will never substitute for His real, lasting solution. Help me draw my life from Him. Feed me completely with You.

It's only by Jesus's marvelous gift I come to You now. Amen

JOHN 15:1, 5

*I am the true vine, and My Father is the gardener.
I am the vine; you are the branches. If a man abide
in Me and I in him, he will bear much fruit;
apart from Me you can do nothing.*

Dear Heavenly Father,

I come to You trusting You know what's best for me. Left to my own devices, I'd become rotten fruit of no use to anybody. You have a clear agenda in mind for me. You long for me to be more like Your Son, Jesus. That process is as individual as I am. Some seasons in this journey will be more painful than others, but You are in control of each one of them. Guide me each step of the way.

Jesus promised to graft me into His vine so I can draw from His strength. I need this source of energy to continue in my battle. I'm too limited in my own resources. I need Your guidance to direct me and Your power to help me overcome my obstacles. Thank You for this gift to aid in my life as Your child. My sinful nature is too much for me to overcome alone. Empower me in each battle I fight.

Pruning sounds so painful for me to bear, but I know You'll only take off what needs to be removed. Your purpose is my best. I do want to be the best I can be as Your adopted child. Discipline isn't a good feeling, but it is necessary. Chastise me when I need it. Remove any hindrances that entangle me as I run this race for You. Enlighten me in each decision I make.

Abundant fruit is my ultimate desire. I really do want to bring You as much as I can. The best quality fruit is my goal. I leave the quantity up to You. Some people will bear more fruit than others. Help me glory in each ones produce for You, even if my amount appears small in comparison. You know what each of us is capable of. Let me be satisfied with that. Be glorified in each yield that I bring.

I ask this in Jesus awesome name. Amen

I AM I AM

When Moses conversed with the bush that didn't burn,
"Who are You that sends me?" This is what he yearned.
"I Am." No two words could say it much better.
A fuller response would take a long letter.
A babe was born to a virgin named Mary.
I Am came down in a form we could carry.
The man He became was bold and audacious.
His claims could only come from one named Jesus.
I Am the bread of life for all to partake.
Sustain you forever and ever each day.
I Am the light of the world that shines in dark
places you hide sins and stains from your heart.
I Am the door of the sheep pen to protect
all of my lambs until pastures I direct.
I Am the Good Shepherd My life I lay down.
This step I must take to one day get a crown.
I Am resurrection and life to each one
who claims Me their Savior and God's only Son.
I Am the only way to God and His throne.
The one truth and life I now declare known.
I Am the true vine abide as my branches.
Draw your strength from Me so your fruit won't be less.
There's Jesus in two words most precious and pure.
No other can match Him of that I am sure.

TIMES AND SEASONS

ECCLESIASTES 3:1-2

There is a time for everything, and a season for every activity under heaven: a time to be born and a time to die, a time to plant and a time to uproot.

Dear Heavenly Father,

I come to You in need of guidance. My world is such a chaos of confusion. Oftentimes I don't know if I'm coming or going, perhaps both. But where I'm heading is the objective of my life I need to discover. Without Your hand steering me, I'll be lost. That's the only thing I'm confident of. Give me Your word, please. A sense of purpose is what I seek. Show me Your direction for me.

Your word, of course, I need to seek Your Word first. Keep reminding me of this vital intake for my life. The Bible should be read and meditated on as much as I breathe. You preserved the scriptures for my sustenance. This isn't a choice I should neglect. This needs to be a core part of my existence. Renew a hunger and thirst for Your words deep within me. Ground me in Your guidance for me.

Life on this planet consists of beginnings and endings. There is a time to be born and a time to plant. These are tender times that require preparations to ensure success. Fortify my resolve to take the best steps to foster the proper atmosphere for a foundation I can build upon. Just like prenatal care and cultivating a field are important help me approach each undertaking with this attitude. Gird me for the work of preparation.

Death is a part of my existence I try to avoid as much as possible. That's not an option You've given me. Brace me for the inevitable when the time comes for loved ones to enter the next phase of life. Yeah, death isn't really an ending but a new beginning. Just because I'm not allowed to see that part of my existence doesn't mean it isn't real. Brace me for this slap of reality.

Help me know when I need to uproot something in my life that's holding me back. Give me the resolve to carry on into my future unobstructed. Bring people in my life who'll tell me the truth about what needs to change. Use Your Spirit to show me what has to go as I read Your truths. Give me the determination to become more like Jesus Christ in all I do. Guide me as to what needs to change.

It's only because of Jesus's sacrifice for me I can come to You now. Amen

ECCLESIASTES 3:1, 3

There is a time for everything, and a season for every activity under heaven: a time to kill and a time to heal, a time to tear down and a time to build,

Dear Heavenly Father,

I come to you full of questions. My life is getting more complicated the more I read Your words. Following You can seem like a jumble of contradictions. I know You are truth, so I trust You. The Bible is my guidebook. I study it to get to know You and what You expect from me. Your ways are so much higher than my ways. I can't come close to comprehending Your thoughts. Calm me as I try to understand You.

I read that You are love. Now I read there is a time to kill. The contradiction holds two seemingly opposite positions together at the same time. What would a perfectly holy God want to kill? Evil is the only thing I can think of. You cannot live with evil, so it must be done away with. War brings a time to kill in order to fulfill a mission. Give me Your supreme wisdom to determine when this needs to occur. Guide me as I put this into practice.

The time after a war is a difficult time. Raw emotions are so tender. Hate is at its height. Healing is so far from everyone's mind. But it's what You call for. Like a cut in skin, healing is a gradual process that takes time. Rushing back to normal too soon can cause more damage than we began with. Emotional healing requires much care and patience. Use me as I attempt to heal my neighbors and myself.

There are idols in my life that need to be torn down before You can use me to tear anyone else's idols down. Help me concentrate my efforts on what I can replace in my own life. Give me insights and wisdom on how best to accomplish this goal. Use Your word to let me see what I need to build in their place so I can be a better child of You. Prepare me for Your work by fixing myself first.

I ask this in the name of Jesus who died and rose again to mediate for me now. Amen

ECCLESIASTES 3:1, 4

There is a time for everything, and a season
for everything under heaven.
A time to weep and a time to laugh, a time
to mourn and a time to dance,

Dear Heavenly Father,

I come to You with tear-stained cheeks and a smile. You greet me with a reassuring grin as You lift me on Your lap. As the One who created me, You know better than anybody how my emotions can play havoc with my life. Being made in Your image means You also have times of mourning and celebrations. Jesus enjoyed weddings and was fully involved at funerals. Help me embrace my likeness to You.

Tears are too familiar sometimes. Life sends one curve ball after another. Tests seem to pile up rather than allowing time to recuperate from one before the next wave hits. I so long to be like Jesus as He slept in a storm-tossed boat while those around Him panicked. I can't reach that level of peace without these tests and stretching. Strengthen me to become more like Your Son.

Times of laughter are such stress-reducing moments. You know I need those from time to time. Thank You for laughter and joy. Without those, I'd lose hope. Without hope, I'd wither and die like a plant without water. Continue to bring lighthearted moments along to sustain me. Help me see humor around me in the mundane things of life. Lift me up with laughter.

Dancing is an event I too often refrain from. I'm too self-conscious to be that conspicuous. Give me occasions to be like King David and remove my outer garb to fully embrace a moment with You. Return to me that childlike burst of happy dance joy You designed me to have. I believe You dance too every time a sinner becomes Your child. Use me to bring people into Your family.

It's only because of the sorrow Jesus endured on the cross I can come before You now. Amen

ECCLESIASTES 3:1, 5

There is a time for everything, and a season for every activity under heaven: a time to scatter stones and a time to gather them, a time to embrace and a time to refrain.

Dear Heavenly Father,

I come to You in all seriousness today. I seek Your wisdom as I traverse this jagged trail called life. My steps are tenuous as I attempt to guide others along the narrow way. Your holiness calls for decisive action at times. Fortunately I live on the grace side of the cross, and I'm not called upon to take drastic measures to assure compliance with Your laws. Help me help others.

There are times in reading the Bible I need to step back and think about what the writer of that scripture was thinking. This is one of those times. Stones aren't used for much these days, maybe decorative landscaping. But in Old Testament times, they were either building material or tools of judgment. I think the latter option is what Solomon had in mind here. Guide me in reading Your Word.

I bring to mind the incident in Jesus's earthly life where they brought an adulterous woman before Him for judgment. The condemning stones were scattered on the ground as Jesus's accusation struck its mark in those judges' hearts. There's a time for grace to give way to punishment. Grant me the wisdom to know when each must come into play. Use me to love others.

An embrace can end a lifetime of sin as easily as a sentence of death. Often what the sinner really seeks is acceptance. Use me to reach out in love and bring hurting souls into Your kingdom. Help me lead them into Your Word to guide them onto the path of righteousness and forgiveness. Your kingdom will be occupied by forgiven sinners. Remind me of this fact.

Help me know when such compassion is going to only be used as an excuse for more sinning. There are those who don't want to give up their sinful life. They merely want me to accept their sin as moral and normal. That's not what Jesus taught. He told the woman to sin no more. I believe she did exactly that. Steer me clear of people who want to use me as an acceptance of their sin. Keep me wise to the truth.

I ask for this wisdom in the power of Jesus's name. Amen

ECCLESIASTES 3:1, 6

There is a time for everything, and a season for every activity under heaven: a time to search and a time to give up, a time to keep and a time to throw away.

Dear Heavenly Father,

I come to You with a sore neck and aching arms. I've spent so much time and energy looking for things and grabbing stuff that I'm at a conundrum as to what to do next. You pull me on Your lap and rub my neck. I hear Your voice in my ear, "Look up to Me for your happiness. Release your possessions and give Me a hug." As I do, my tension abates and peace returns. Keep reminding me of Your sufficiency.

It's not that searching and keeping are bad. It's the priority I place on what I'm seeking and finding that need assessment. Give me a heavenly perspective so I concentrate my efforts on building Your kingdom. My happiness should take a back seat to Your assignments for me. Help me seek the lost and guard Your truth in my heart. Keep focusing me on Your Word.

There are proper times to release certain things in my life. Some friendships need to be ended. Give me wisdom to recognize those that drain me with discouragement and drag me away from You. Grant me the strength to walk away from these people so I can concentrate on those who need me and/or build me up. Help me recognize those who don't want to change. Keep using me to love others.

Some physical items are a weight on my life that should be discarded. Give me wisdom to know when to give my stuff away to those who truly need it more than I do. Family history and emotional attachment are difficult things to let go of. But when someone else can benefit from these things, give me the courage to release them into Your plan for the benefit of others. Keep guiding me to be Your heart.

I ask this in the mighty name of Jesus who kept His focus by throwing away an earthly kingdom. Amen

ECCLESIASTES 3:1, 7A

There is a time for everything,
and a season for every activity under heaven:
a time to tear and a time to mend.

Dear Heavenly Father,

I come to You with my clothes in tatters. This battlefield of life is quite a challenge to get through without some discomfort. Perfection will only be discovered when I come into Your eternal presence. You brush the dust off me as You set me on Your lap. A kiss to my forehead melts me into Your shoulder. My soul again finds peace and comfort. Thank You for Your strength and love.

You inspect my clothes then gently rip the sleeves off just above the elbow. The excess material is discarded in the garbage. My arms are now free to move about unencumbered. Perhaps I can fight better now. Grant me wisdom as to what other things, habits, or relationships need to be thrown away to help me better serve You. Thank You for Your kindness and guidance.

With needle and thread, You carefully repair my pants. The embarrassing rips are fixed first then the ones that protect my skin. Yes, I still need a layer of protection from thorns and briers. The material is enough for that mission. Let me know which relationships will help me by fixing them. I need some friends by my side in this fight. Thank You for Your skill and patience.

As I march off to my next assignment, I glance back and smile at Your wink. I know You won't leave me alone in the battle. You'll give me the endurance, wisdom, fortitude, and strength to carry out the tasks laid before me. The tearing and mending that need to be done are what I'll concentrate on now. Thank You for Your gifts and faithfulness.

It's only by the bridge built by Jesus's matchless sacrifice I come to You now. Amen

ECCLESIASTES 3:1, 7B

There is a time for everything,
and a season for every activity under heaven:
a time to be silent and a time to speak.

Dear Heavenly Father,

    I come to You with my head held low. I'm ashamed of what I said recently. I wish for a do-over so I can correct my blunder, but I know that's not an option. I'm unsure as to whether You'll still take me in. My mind can't comprehend how You can forgive me. You come across the room, pick me up, and set me on Your lap. Remind me Your love is unconditional.

    I hear the phrase "silence is golden," but I have a hard time putting it into practice. Guard my tongue against hasty judgments and accusations. Give me a peace that others make mistakes too. It's not my place to set them in their place. Quiet my thoughts and my tongue when I'm prone to jump in with my harsh words. Remind me You are the ultimate judge.

    Silence isn't always the best option, though. There are times I need to say something in defense of the defenseless. I need Your wisdom to know when these times are and what I'm to say. Give me the fewest amount of words to get my point across. Let me get to the heart of the matter without muddying the waters further. Remind me there are times to stand up.

I come back to needing wisdom here. Help me pause and think before I open my mouth to speak. Sometimes my presence is simply the best thing to do. Words aren't always necessary. But when they are needed, use me to comfort and heal more than anything. Sometimes it's the people listening in who'll gain the most from my conversation. Remind me I represent You.

Give me this strength in Jesus's precious name. Amen

ECCLESIASTES 3:1, 8A

There is a time for everything, and a
season for every activity under heaven:
a time to love and a time to hate.

Dear Heavenly Father,

My confusion level is running high again today. I search Your eyes for answers. Your smile begins in Your eyes as You lift me on Your lap. Your peace fills me, but the confusion remains. How can I love and hate at the same time? These emotions appear at odds with each other, yet You tell me to feel both. Help me understand Your ways.

When I close my eyes, I see Jesus talking to the Samaritan woman, then overturning the money changers' tables at the temple. The contrast is so remarkable the lesson is clear. It's not the feeling I'm to concentrate on but the object of the emotion. Jesus reached out with grace and compassion as He answered the woman's questions. Help me love as Jesus loved.

The money changers weren't the ones Jesus harmed at the temple that day. It was their tables He toppled. The source of His hatred was the deed they committed. Where they set up business was to be a place of prayer, not commerce. He hated their location of exchange, not them. His wrath was directed at the implements of exchange. Help me be wise in my hatred.

People are to be the focus of my love. Sin is to be the focus of my hatred. The two can coexist in harmony. Grant me wisdom as I live out this dichotomy. Some will be confused by my actions, or they'll try to confuse others as to my motives. Help me demonstrate Your love for souls and hatred for sin in this world that sees everything as gray. Help me be Your ambassador.

It's only by Jesus's incredible gift of love given on the cross I come to You for wisdom. Amen

ECCLESIASTES 3:1, 8B

There is a time for everything,
and a season for every activity under heaven:
a time for war and a time for peace.

Dear Heavenly Father,

I come to You today in shock from all the fighting I witness in the news. I guess wars occur all the time. It's just the technology available that lets me see them in my home. I wish for a tranquil world to live in. Harmony is so precious yet so hard to find. The echo of Eve's teeth breaking the skin of that forbidden fruit is still heard among us. Give assurance that You are still in control.

It makes sense that a country defending itself has every right to go to war. The country invading them is the one I'm concerned with. Why can't we agree to accept each other's right to exist and dwell together as neighbors? Religious and spiritual reasons are often given for these conflicts. The struggle between good and evil endures. Remind me that Your side wins in the end.

Skirmishes on our own borders are the most difficult to understand. When underlying tensions explode over a brief encounter, I see just how fragile peace actually is. I pray for cooler heads and calm leadership to prevail in these instances. Help us understand each other and come to a mutual acceptance of each other's place in this world. Step in and create a better atmosphere for us to live in.

Peace, it's such a small word. Perhaps that's why it's so delicate and hard to keep alive. Toddlers will fight over a small toy, adults over a chunk of ground. Help us nurture the peace we have so it thrives as long as possible. True, lasting peace won't exist until You set up Your eternal kingdom filled with Your adopted children. Use me to bring others into that precious time of peace.

I ask this in Jesus's glorious name. Amen

THE HALL OF FAITH

HEBREWS 11:1-2

Now faith is being sure of what we hope for
and certain of what we do not see.
This is what the ancients were commended for.

Dear Heavenly Father,

I stand before You at the edge of a new day. I peer down this corridor of faith and wonder if I have what it takes to be in the presence of these giants of faith. Your smile and wink assure me I am in the same stratosphere with these people simply because I acknowledge You exist. I've never seen You with my physical eyes but know You're real. Keep me focused on You.

The Bible is the most unusual book ever composed, with sixty-six books written over vast centuries with a common theme: my relationship with You. Thank You for preserving the account of Your dealings with people like me through the years. I find hope and comfort in knowing You care about each of us on a personal level. Remind me of Your love for me. I read that Your desire to restore a personal relationship is so important to You that You became one of us to give Your very life for me. No greater love could ever be displayed. Jesus not only died for me, He lived an exemplary life for me to emulate. Grant me the wisdom and fortitude to walk closely in His footsteps. May people see Him in me as much as possible. Help me copy the Master.

You've blessed me with stories to help others see You too. Guide me as I fulfill this mission. Give me the best words, characters, and themes to convey Your truths to edify and educate. Use Your Holy Spirit to enlighten dark eyes to You. Change the course of eternal destinies by what I write and what they read. I lay my writing before You now as an offering of love and devotion. Use me as Your instrument.

It's in the all-powerful name of Jesus I claim You and Your promises now. Amen

HEBREWS 11:3

By faith we understand that the universe
was formed at God's command, so that what is
seen was not made out of what was visible.

Dear Heavenly Father,

I come to You in absolute awe. I'm talking awe to the fullest extent of the meaning of the term. When I try to wrap my mind around the origins of everything I see I'm blown away by You. There is nothing in my existence that wasn't made by Your will. Yet You chose me as Your child. I'm honored and humbled to be associated with You. Thank You for reaching me.

Scientists have been searching for answers as to exactly what holds everything in place. Their lack of faith pushes them to see the invisible. They could save themselves such folly if they'd merely believe Your Word. Even they admit Your existence when they call the substance that holds atoms together "the God particle." Use me to spread the word of Your existence. Thank You for including me.

Some try to divert people away from You by offering theories of their own making. Others push such suppositions as truth to the youth of today. I know the truth can't be hidden from You. The day they bow their knees to You will be eye-opening to say the least. By then, it will be too late for them to choose to believe in Your gift of an existence with You. Thank You for enlightening me.

You need me to tell others of Your existence and power. I accept the role of Your ambassador. Give me the words to speak and write that convey Your love and truth to a dying generation. Help me reach out when needed to love with actions and a listening ear. Empower me to encourage the hurting and rescue the silent victims. Thank You for using me.

It's only because of the awesome gift given by Jesus I can come to You now. Amen

HEBREWS 11:4

*By faith Abel offered God a better sacrifice
than Cain did. By faith he was commended as a
righteous man, when God spoke well of his offerings.
And by faith he still speaks, even though he is dead.*

Dear Heavenly Father,

I come to You with the first martyr on my mind. I'm told very little about this man in scripture. But I know enough to know he loved You. He gave his best to You when You called for it. Cain apparently held his best back. Let that thought sink into my heart as I live out my salvation. Help me strive to give You my best at all times. Remain my number one.

Abel didn't know his life would end with no offspring. I'm sure he thought his life would run its course in the natural flow with him being a father of many. The tragedy that ended his life shocked everyone. He still left a legacy in his wake. This one offering he gave You is my lesson of a lifetime. May I focus on the project You've given me now. Remain my source of inspiration.

I don't know how many books, devotions, or articles I'll have published. I may only have time for one offering to You. I long for a lengthy writing career with many bylines. Your plans aren't always my plans. Help me put my efforts into each piece as though it'll be my last one, because one time it will be. Remain my audience of one.

My goal is for You to speak well of me and what I do. I'd love to be commended as righteous in Your eyes. I know that's impossible for me to attain in my efforts. That's why You came as Jesus to stand in that gap of sin-filled separation. Still, if it did depend on my life's work...would You be pleased with me? Would You accept me like You did Abel? Remain my aspiration.

It's only, and always, because of Jesus's sacrifice I come before You now. Amen

HEBREWS 11:5-6

By faith Enoch was taken from this life, so that he did not experience death; he could not be found, because God had taken him away. For before he was taken, he was commended as one who pleased God. And without faith it is impossible to please God, because anyone who comes to Him must believe that He exists and that He rewards those who earnestly seek Him.

Dear Heavenly Father,

I come to You in wonderful awe. I just read about the first person to be raptured from this life into Your presence. I eagerly await that same possibility for me. Many accept that will be the next event in Your prophetic timetable. Now that I know it's been done before, I can be even more assured You'll do it again. Come quickly, Lord!

I'm told in Genesis 5:24 that Enoch walked with God. He had a personal relationship with the Creator. I have the ability to share that experience as Enoch did. My adoption into Your spiritual family insures my coming into Your presence as well. How close I come to You before then is up to me. Walk closely children.

I'm amazed Enoch had such a relationship with no scripture or example to follow. I have both the Bible and Jesus's life to guide me along. Your placing the Holy Spirit's life in me to lead me makes me all the more impressed with his walk. Keep me mindful of my responsibility to follow You. Lead boldly, Spirit.

I long to please You too, God. Give me a heart that desires Your smile in everything I do. Guide my steps to mimic Jesus's example. Help me love those around me as He did. Keep me mindful of the reward You have for me. I long to have crowns awaiting that I can lay at Jesus's feet in the kingdom to come. Reward honestly, Father.

It's in the glorious name of Jesus, I stand in Your presence now. Amen

HEBREWS 11:7

By faith Noah, when warned about things
not yet seen, in holy fear built an ark to save his family.
By his faith he condemned the world and became
heir of the righteousness that comes by faith.

Dear Heavenly Father,

    I come to You with a stark contrast of a familiar children's story on my mind. You pull me into a warm embrace before setting me on Your lap for my time of communion with You. The consequences of sin are severe. Too often I water that truth down so I don't offend people. That's not my role. Is it? Remind me of the battle I fight.

    I prefer to think about the people and animals who were saved from the disaster rather than those who refused to believe You. Use me to present Your offer of salvation from the coming end of this world as we know it and the establishment of Your kingdom yet to come. People need to hear of Your love and acceptance of them. Strengthen me for this battle I'm in.

I'm not told how many times Noah may have doubted what you called him to do. I can only guess how often he nearly quit this ridiculous building project You laid out for him to accomplish. Grant me his perseverance as I write Your stories for others to read. Give me Your words to touch hurting hearts. Equip me for this battle of ink.

I must march on, no matter what obstacles I face. The odds may be stacked against me. The enemy may seem too strong and/or numerous for me to face alone. If Peter can walk on water, why can't I fly when You call me to? Your Spirit within me can do mighty things, too mighty for my puny mind to imagine. Use me to win this battle for souls.

It's only because of Jesus's great sacrifice and mighty love I come before You now. Amen

HEBREWS 11:8

By faith Abraham, when called to go to a place he would later receive as an inheritance, obeyed and went, even though he did not know where he was going.

Dear Heavenly Father,

I come to You today in search of direction. I feel lost in this journey You called me to. I want to know the outcome so I can have confidence to continue. You lift me on Your lap and whisper, "My grace is sufficient for you." My pout turns to peace as I accept Your gift of love. Continue to use me.

You display the life of Abraham to me. He didn't know where he was going or how it would turn out. His faith kept him on track with a few missteps. He never saw the promise fulfilled in his lifetime. Yet his descendants live there today. Your timing seldom matches my timing. Continue to guide me.

Give me the words You want people to read. It really isn't about me. It's all You, or it should be. Remind me this life isn't about my happiness. I'm called to carry a cross daily. That cross is as individual as I am. Let me be the instrument in Your orchestra as You conduct this symphony. Continue to supply me.

The battlefield of my mind and heart is so busy. Thoughts creep in when I least expect them to. My attention is diverted so easily from Your goal for me. Steel my determination and focus my attention on pleasing You in all I do. Give me the grit to take each step as I further Your kingdom. Continue to strengthen me.

It's completely on the sufficiency of Jesus Christ I come to You now. Amen

HEBREWS 11:9-10

By faith Abraham made his home in the promised land like a stranger in a foreign country; he lived in tents, as did Isaac and Jacob, who were heirs with him of the same promise. For he was looking forward to the city with foundations, whose architect and builder is God.

Dear Heavenly Father,

I come to You with an ache in my heart. I'm reminded of my first time at summer camp. Homesickness is the familiar pang. My time with You eases this discomfort, but I know it's only temporary. Your warm hug tells me You understand. Your smile assures me this is normal. I'm designed with a God-shaped hole in my heart. Keep me longing for You.

Adam and Eve were the first people You made. They had a personal relationship with You in Eden. Their disobedience broke that bond. A spiritual death has plagued those of us who came after them. I grope for ways to end this pain within. Temporary fixes are all I've come up with. Nothing lasts. Keep me hungry for righteousness.

Most people don't know where to find any real, lasting peace. They join causes that make sense only to be taken advantage of by the leaders. They try pleasure as a means of escape. Still, they come up empty. They evade reality through drugs of many types. That hole remains in them. Give me words of hope.

You knew of only one true fix for the mess I'm in. So You became one of us in the man Jesus. You lived as You want me to live. You died as my substitute to sign my adoption paper with Your own blood. I now have hope for a brighter future. My eternal home is assured. I'm ready to be called home. Thank You for calling me Yours.

It's not enough for me to hoard this gift. Sure, I'm happy to have a place at Your heavenly table. But shouldn't I tell others of this amazing opportunity? It's available for them too. Give me the words and actions that point people to You. Let them see echoes of Jesus in me. Use me as an adoption agent for You.

It's only because of the bridge Jesus built with the cross I come to You now. Amen

HEBREWS 11:11-12

By faith Abraham, even though he was past age—and Sarah herself was barren—was enabled to become a father because he considered Him faithful who had made the promise. And so from this one man, and he as good as dead, came descendants as numerous as the stars in the sky and as countless as the sand on the seashore.

Dear Heavenly Father,

I come to You scratching my head. How can a couple become a family at such an old age? The answer can only be YOU. As Gabriel told Mary, the word *impossible* isn't in Your vocabulary. The Creator of the universe is still in control of every detail in this life. Remind me of Your sovereignty.

I need that reassurance now. Some things in my life seem beyond repair. A relationship is broken with no sign of restoration. A career appears ending with no prospect of advancement or stability. My health is in question with a prognosis of a grim outcome. Remind me of Your concern.

I live in a broken world. The closer I reach the end of this era, the worse it'll be. This spiritual battle is reaching a climax. You turned the tide in this war when You took on a human body in the line of this elderly couple. Jesus gave His life so I can be restored in my relationship with You. Remind me of Your love.

My focus needs to be You. My love needs to draw strength from You. My next breath needs to come from You. My future needs to be guided by You. I need You as I reach out to this dying world. This generation is running away from You. Give me the words that will turn them around. Remind me of Your power.

I thank You for this intercession of prayer in my life. Grow my dependence on asking You for wisdom, strength, and courage to continue this journey I'm on. You placed me in this generation for a reason. Help me fulfill that mission for me. Remind me of Your provision.

It's only because of Abraham's descendant, Jesus, that I come before You now. Amen

HEBREWS 11:13-16

All these people were still living by faith when they died. They did not receive the things promised; they only saw them and welcomed them from a distance. And they admitted that they were aliens and strangers on earth. People who say such things show that they are looking for a country of their own. If they had been thinking of the country they had left, they would have had opportunity to return. Instead, they were longing for a better country—a heavenly one. Therefore God is not ashamed to be called their God, for He has prepared a city for them.

Dear Heavenly Father,

I skip into Your presence today and dance to Your outstretched arms. Your laughter tells me I'm home—I belong here. This union is so blessed and rich. My heart is always lighter when I see You. I think Yours is too. The burdens of this world fall off my back as You lift me up. Embrace me with Your love.

You pull out my adoption papers to show me this transaction is real. My tears fall on the bottom of the page when I notice the name of Jesus is still a deep red. It took His blood to fulfill all the obligations of sonship for me. I don't think I ponder the price that was paid often enough. Remind me of Your love.

One look into Your smiling eyes and I'm assured Your love is so grand that this was no small sacrifice for You. You becoming one of us to live as we do and experience all we do was necessary. How else could You bridge the gap between us? Jesus touched so many lives one at a time as an example for me. Help me emulate Your love.

Jesus's tears in the garden, the cup that couldn't pass, the anguish was so deep. He knew You couldn't abide with sin. He knew, for the first time in all eternity, He would be removed from Your presence for a time when my sin became His. That separation was almost too much for even Him to bear, but He did. Ground me in this truth.

The precious promise I strive for is that Jesus is building a future home with You—a place where You will be the light; a home with no darkness, shadows, or secrets. I'll know and be known. This eternal dwelling will be mine with You. Thank You for this hope that drives me onward. Strengthen me with Your love.

It's always and only because of King Jesus I come to You now. Amen

HEBREWS 11:17-19

By faith Abraham, when God tested him, offered Isaac as a sacrifice. He who had received the promises was about to sacrifice his one and only son, even though God had said to him, "It is through Isaac that your offspring will be reckoned." Abraham reasoned that God could raise the dead, and figuratively speaking, he did receive Isaac back from the dead.

Dear Heavenly Father,

I come to You perplexed as I'm reminded of one of the most controversial passages in all the Bible. You specifically told Abraham to kill his only son for no reason other than to test his trust in You. How could You be so cruel? Aren't You the God of love and mercy, grace and forgiveness? Teach me Your purpose.

Had this long- awaited son become some sort of idol to Abraham? Was his heart focused on the one promised to carry on the promise rather than the one who gave the promise? Why did You demand such a severe act of obedience? Your silence on these questions is deafening. Show me Your plan.

Deepen my relationship with You so I'm willing to take extreme measures for You. Grant me the boldness of Abraham to act outrageously. You need to be my top priority, my ultimate focus, the desire of my heart. Help me hear Your voice clearly in all I do. Grant me Your priority.

Abraham knew the miracle it took to bring Isaac into existence. He trusted Your word that a nation would come from this son. He reasoned You would bring him back to life after this sacrifice, even though You had yet to perform such a miracle. His experience propelled him forward. Keep me on Your path.

I'm reminded of another one and only son who did die. He gave His life freely for me. You did bring Him back to life to show Your power over death. Your outrageous love compelled You to die in my place to fulfill my adoption into Your family. Your grace is completed with this obedience. Prepare my eternal home for me.

This gift is too grand to be hoarded. I must tell others. Thank You for gifting me with words. Give me stories that focus people on You. Use Your Spirit to touch their hearts to change course and take an extreme step of faith into Your family. Help me "reproduce" Your children.

It's because of the outrageous act of obedience of Jesus I come to You now, Father. Amen

HEBREWS 11:20-21

By faith Isaac blessed Jacob and Esau in regard to their future. By faith Jacob, when he was dying, blessed each of Joseph's sons, and worshiped as he leaned on the top of his staff.

Dear Heavenly Father,

I come to You with a longing and a question. When did people stop giving blessings? This practice holds so much hope and expectation. Why don't we want that for our children? Give me wisdom as I attempt to bring this back into play with my own family. Guide my words to hope.

As our perfect spiritual Father, You gave us a blessing while You were on earth as Jesus. John preserved those words for us in his gospel. John 17:20–26 were His hopes and dreams for us. He prayed for unity and love as a display of proof of our adoption into Your family. Use my life to love.

As any good parent does, Jesus longed for me to be with Him. He promised me that He's building a place for me to spend eternity with Him. He'll stop at nothing to assure this takes place. He even sacrificed His own life to confirm this transaction transpires. Compel my heart to faith.

Today's verse tells me Jacob worshipped as he blessed his grandchildren. So this act of giving hope to the next generation is a means of worshipping You, too. Another way to worship You can only lift my heart higher. Drive my desires to give this blessing to others and You. Steer my soul to obedience.

Isaac and Jacob gave specific blessings. They knew the hearts of their families. Help me be a good student of those I love. Guide my eyes to see Your plans for them by their words and actions. Move by Your Spirit to bring them into Your family too. Use me as Your tool of salvation. Draw their lives to You.

It's only because of Jesus's desire and faithfulness I come to You now. Amen

HEBREWS 11:22

By faith Joseph, when his end was near,
spoke about the exodus of the Israelites from
Egypt and gave instructions about his bones.

Dear Heavenly Father,

I come to You amazed again. The life of Joseph is such an incredible account. This man endured such misunderstanding, hatred, false accusations, and persecution, yet he never lost sight of You. His life was completely sold out to You. His faith was immense. May I emulate his example.

He looked with hope to the future when he remembered how You worked in his past. He recognized You never left him. As he remained in prison, he must have wondered where You were. Looking back, he saw Your hand in the timing of it all. Your schedule seldom matches my timetable. May You grow my patience.

The wicked intentions of his brothers were even a part of Your plan. You turned their evil into good for them. Nobody saw You in that act of hatred, yet You were there all along. Israel laid the foundation of trust in his eleventh son well. The tests were just beginning. May I trust Your heart.

Joseph's rise to power took numerous turns. The humility he endured never left him as he forgave those who meant to end him. He knew Your promise was for this family to live in the land promised to the fathers. He desired for his bones to be buried next to his Abba. May I long for You.

Jesus's life had many parallels to Joseph. He too suffered much misunderstanding, hatred, false accusations, and persecution. His anguish in the garden showed His longing to remain in His Abba's presence. Yet He endured the cross for me. I believe His kingdom is coming. May I rejoice with You.

It's in the unselfish giving of Jesus's life that I come to You now. Amen

HEBREWS 11:23

By faith Moses' parents hid him for three months after he was born, because they saw he was no ordinary child, and they were not afraid of the king's edict.

Dear Heavenly Father,

I come to You amazed yet again. Today's verse puts the spotlight on two people not even named. Moses's parents knew their son was special somehow. You must have stepped in by Your Holy Spirit and told them silently. You also gave them a boldness to go against the "power" of the land and hide their son You gave them. Speak to me, too.

Looking back, I can easily see You in Moses's life. The way Pharaoh's daughter took him in and raised him as her own is astonishing. He was given an education no Hebrew had the opportunity for in over four hundred years. That education was put to good use when he wrote the first five books of the Bible. Grant me wisdom, now.

As a writer, I've been given a special opportunity to grow Your kingdom. You've planted ideas and characters in my mind that have to come out. Guide my thoughts as I birth these stories to shine the light back on You in multiple ways. Shape my passion as I pursue which avenue to use to bring them to life. Direct my path, daily.

When I think of how Jesus gave His all for me, I long to reciprocate by giving my best back to You. Put me in contact with the best people to help me edit, illustrate, publish, or whatever else I need for my stories to shine. Provide the funding for self-publishing options as those options are advanced in Your will. Build my team, strong.

I live during a time when being one of Your followers is becoming increasingly difficult. Some people are paying with their lives for proclaiming to be Your child. Others are simply turning their backs on You and following the worldly lusts of self-interest. Give me a boldness that can't be ignored. Indwell me voraciously, indeed.

It's because of that special child born that first Christmas who died for me, Jesus Christ, I come to You now. Amen

HEBREWS 11:24-26

By faith Moses, when he had grown up, refused to be known as the son of Pharaoh's daughter. He chose to be mistreated along with the people of God rather than to enjoy the pleasures of sin for a short time. He regarded disgrace for the sake of Christ as of greater value than the treasures of Egypt, because he was looking ahead to his reward.

Dear Heavenly Father,

I come to You shaking my head. I admire the strength of perseverance Moses lived in his life. He had it all by the world's measure—wealth, pleasure, leisure, royalty—yet he walked away from it for You. When he discovered he was one of Your chosen people, he stepped into the sandals of a slave. Help me grasp this mentality.

Moses could have continued to live a lie. Nobody would have faulted him for it. He could have ruled Your people, but You had other plans. You chose for him to lead Your people to the land promised to their forefathers. Somehow he saw that plan. He knew they didn't belong in Egypt. Help me catch that vision.

My whole world is bent on pleasure. I carry little entertainment gadgets in my pocket. Distractions surround me to trap me here rather than to spend time with You. I could easily fall in with the masses and absorb this lifestyle, but You have a plan for me to lead people to Your home. Help me shake these bonds.

My stories are *NOT* to be used to bring attention to me, as much as some people want me to twist it that way. I long to show You to others. You've given me a vision to spread Your message of love and hope by story. Use me. Give me Your words. Guide my stories to reflect You. Help me show Your heart.

I may not make enough money from my writing to live on that income alone. The small amount of fame I see likely won't disrupt my life much. If I do get notoriety and wealth from writing, keep me grounded to Your purpose. Help me reflect Your light so it outshines any spotlights others put on me. Help me remember Your plan.

It's only because of Jesus's ultimate sacrifice I come before You now. Amen

HEBREWS 11:27-28

By faith Moses left Egypt, not fearing the king's anger; he persevered because he saw Him who is invisible. By faith he kept the Passover and the sprinkling of blood, so that the destroyer of the firstborn would not touch the firstborn of Israel.

Dear Heavenly Father,

I come to You from my visible world into Your invisible presence. I see You too, much as Moses did, not with my physical eyes but with spiritual eyes. The aspect of this relationship that surprises me most is that You want to spend time with me. Then again, why else would You pay so high a price to adopt me as Your own. Thank You for making me family.

Moses held a reverential fear of You. He didn't run from Pharaoh to escape his wrath. He ran to You. After forty years of solitude, You spoke to Him. You used this frail man in mighty ways simply because You chose to. I also feel unworthy to be an instrument of value for Your service. Use me anyway. Thank You for using me mightily.

The Passover was unprecedented. Never before had only the firstborn from every family been in jeopardy. There was no time for debate over the matter. Fast action was called for to avoid the cataclysm. The unsanitary smearing of blood on the door posts made no sense, but that's what You called for. Thank You for shaking me awake.

My times are perilous, indeed. Beheadings are too common now. This spiritual battle is reaching a climax. Satan knows his end is near, so he's pulling out all the stops. Use me to give the battle cry to Your people. There's not much time before You close the door on further adoptions. Thank You for giving me boldness.

I run into this battle with the blood of Christ smeared on me. I caught it at the foot of the cross. One drop of His blood is all it took to finalize this transaction. I've taken advantage of this union with You. Now use me to tell others so they can benefit from the same relationship I enjoy. Thank You for loving me completely.

It's only because of the bridge Jesus built with His blood I come to You now. Amen

HEBREWS 11:29-30

By faith the people passed through the Red Sea as on dry land; but when the Egyptians tried to do so, they were drowned. By faith the walls of Jericho fell, after the people had marched around them for seven days.

Dear Heavenly Father,

I come to You in complete awe. Your power is incredible. Your will is totally unpredictable. Your judgments are final. Your calls to action can be baffling. Nobody can measure up to You. Anybody who tries to bring You down to their level just doesn't get it. Thank You for including me in Your family. Remain true to You.

You deliberately placed Your people in a predicament where they'd have to depend on You to get them out of it. Imagine their shock when the water of a vast sea drew back so they could escape the Egyptians for good. Imagine the terror of the mighty fighting men when the waters engulfed them. Stay providential for me.

The next generation of Your people saw the seemingly impenetrable walls of the mighty city of Jericho. They obeyed Your command to simply walk around the enemy fortification for a week. You didn't even breathe hard when the walls crumbled into dust. They experienced Your might. Continue to surprise me.

As a writer, I face obstacles to publication that seem impenetrable. The gatekeepers are stingier than ever. Self-publishing is daunting, expensive, and challenging too. Yet You give me stories to change the world one person at a time. As You gave the stories, help me depend on You to bring them to life in Your time. Hold hope for me.

Satan is pursuing me too. He doesn't want me to succeed for You. He tries to discourage, dissuade, distract, and/or whatever method he can come up with to knock me off track. As You stopped the Egyptians cold, bring him to his knees by Your might. Encourage me to continue my journey for You. Steady me on course.

It's in the awesome power Jesus displayed over death I come to You now. Amen

HEBREWS 11:31

By faith the prostitute Rahab, because she welcomed the spies, was not killed with those who were disobedient.

Dear Heavenly Father,

I come to you with my mouth hanging open. You took in a woman most people saw as a sex object and nothing more. Yet You looked past the surface of her life and saw her heart. You always do. You saw her reaction when she encountered Your men. Remind me of Your love.

Rahab's display of reverential fear of You was an astounding show of courage. She stepped up to protect Your men like nobody's business. Her boldness is inspiring. Her bravery is incredible. Her actions came from her heart, the place You see best. Remind me of Your scope.

She jumped at the chance for a new life. She longed for the second chance You offered through Your men. Rahab followed the steps laid out for her to achieve this goal. Then she invited family members to join her. You didn't require much, just faith and obedience. Remind me of Your opportunity.

How odd that tower must have dominated the landscape after the rest of the wall fell. It wasn't that the wall was sturdier there, no. You stayed Your hand to uphold and protect that stronghold for Rahab and her family. Your judgment wasn't directed to that group who feared You. Remind me of Your protection.

When I read Matthew's genealogy of Jesus, I'm struck by the second of four female names in the list. Rahab's life was so important to You her name is preserved as an example to follow. You came for even the worst of those outside of Your chosen race. My mouth falls open once again. Remind me of Your audaciousness.

It's because of my Savior who carried some of Rahab's genes I come to You now. Amen

HEBREWS 12:1

Therefore, since we are surrounded by such a great cloud of witnesses, let us throw off everything that hinders and the sin that so easily entangles, and let us run with perseverance the race marked out for us.

Dear Heavenly Father,

As I come to that time where I anticipate taking down the calendars that have kept me on track for twelve months and replacing them with fresh ones, I'm quite relieved to have survived this year of turmoil and frustrations. Help me release the hurts, the pain, the regrets, and bad memories. Allow me to move on.

I thank You for the relationship I have with You. As my heavenly Father I know Your Holy Spirit resides in me to guide me. You can change my heart and attitudes to make me more like Jesus Christ. I desire that more than anything else. This transformation can be excruciating. Mold me into His image.

Satan will do all he can to make sure I'm not changed by life. He tries to trap me with past weaknesses. Help me not turn back. He tries to divert me to carnal pleasures. Help me stay on

Your track. He tries to get me caught up in prideful thoughts and actions. Help me stay grounded in humility. Strengthen me for the race.

I'm being watched. Whether I know it or not others are keeping a close eye on me. Children naturally want to imitate parents. My friends want part of me to rub off on them. People are searching for someone to lead them. Keep me focused on this fact so I remain deliberate in my actions and attitudes. Focus me on my course.

You have a plan for me. Nobody else's courses matches mine. Keep me from desiring what someone else has that I think I want. Help me remain content with where You have me while staying hungry to reach more people for You. Bring the people that only I can reach for You. Equip me for the task.

It's all because of the transforming power of Jesus Christ I come before You now. Amen

HEBREWS 12:2-3

Let us fix our eyes on Jesus, the author and perfecter of our faith, who for the joy set before Him endured the cross, scorning its shame, and sat down at the right hand of the throne of God. Consider Him who endured such opposition from sinful men, so that you will not grow weary and lose heart.

Dear Heavenly Father,

I bow before Your throne of grace in complete awe. When I remember all You endured so I can be Your child, it astounds me all over again. The cross, the blood, the total disgrace of it all is incredible when I realize Jesus looked to His future and my future with You. Remind me of this love.

What's even more incredible is the fact this was all written out before the earth was formed. You knew that suffering was needed before I did. You wrote the script to come as a baby, grow into a man, and die to renew my relationship with You. Only You as a sinless man could build that bridge. Remind me of this fact.

You could have decided to leave the tree of the knowledge of good and evil out of the Garden of Eden. This would all have been diverted. In Your wisdom, You went ahead with Your plan. This test was needed for people. Would we decide to follow You, or our own lusts? Now You know who truly loves You. Remind me of this test.

I feel the opposition too. Too often I cave in to the requests to remain silent. I take the easy road out to avoid ridicule. I'm sorry for my self- serving attitude. Grant me a new boldness to speak up for You. Give me the words to tell of Your love no matter the personal cost. Remind me of my testimony.

When I read the book of Revelation, I see that Jesus is seated at Your mighty right hand. The Lamb who was slain is the only one qualified to open the judgment scroll that puts an end to man's wickedness. Drive me to bring others to see this reality before it's too late. Remind me of my role.

Lead me onward by the power of Jesus, the Lamb who was slain. Amen

PSALM 23

PSALM 23:1

The Lord is my shepherd, I shall not be in want.

Dear Heavenly Father,

I come to You bewildered and lost. My past is close behind me. My life is a shambles. I need a leader to follow, a role model who has traveled this road before me. You gather me on Your lap and smile. You understand me. You offer Yourself as my guide. My anxiety lessens as You hold me close. Thank You for being there for me.

You offer to be my shepherd. That means I'm to take on the role of a stupid sheep. That analogy fits me to a tee. I too easily follow others who are lost. I set off on my own and quickly find I'm lost. I'm vulnerable to attack when I'm alone. I need one who is much stronger and wiser to lead me. Thank You for guiding me.

As the Creator of everything, You own everything. Your provisions are limitless. Your heart is open to those who long to be used by You. My faith will grow each time You step in to fill a need. I'd prefer to have more than enough. I want what looks appealing and pretty. You know my actual needs. Thank You for meeting my needs.

To follow a true leader means I need to give up control of my life. That is so against my inner being. I think I know what's best for me. I believe I'm the best person to judge my needs. Your wisdom is infinite. Mine is severely lacking. Help me release my grip on my life so You can have Your way with me. Thank You for seeking my best.

The enemy is prowling about seeking to devour me. His roar is loud because he's so close. Your presence keeps him at bay. He knows You are unconquerable. He must get permission from You to attack me as he'd like to. You set a fence around him. Your protection is ever-present. Thank You for Your love and strength.

It's by the power given by the Lamb slain for me, Jesus Christ, I come to You now. Amen

PSALM 23:1A-2A

The LORD is my shepherd. He makes
me lie down in green pastures.

Dear Heavenly Father,

I come to You hungry. I have cravings that must be met. My appetite is insatiable. You smile and nod as I approach. You lift me on Your lap and embrace me in that warm hug of Yours. Of course You understand me. You're the One who made me. Thank You for understanding.

What could satisfy a hungry lamb better than a green pasture? A good shepherd knows where the best forage is for his flock. I know You want what's best for me. Keep me satisfied in the pasture You have set aside for me. Don't let me wander to less fulfilling fields. Thank You for caring.

Some lambs feel the need to run. A good shepherd knows the hard way to keep that type of sheep in safety. He breaks the lamb's leg and splints it up to mend. That little lamb becomes dependent on the shepherd to move it from place to place. Thank You for disciplining.

The sheep who follow the shepherd closest are the ones who've endured the hardship. Their love and trust of the shepherd is built in the turmoil of discipline. They learn dependence in the one who hurt them for their own good. Your discipline is no less needed for me Your child. Thank You for loving.

May I never take for granted the green pasture You have for me. Keep me content in Your plan for me. The pains and turmoil of this life can be excruciating at times. Help me do the best I can with what You've given me. Let me lie down in Your green pasture. Thank You for providing.

It's only and always because of the work done by Jesus Christ I come to You now. Amen

PSALM 23:1A, 2B

The Lord is my shepherd. He leads me beside quiet waters.

Dear Heavenly Father,

My throat is parched as I come to You today. My lips are cracked from the arid land I live in. I've tried everything I can find to slake my thirst. You pull me on Your lap and tuck me into Your embrace. Your warmth fills me from within. How did I ever forget Your inner presence in my soul? Satisfy my longings.

As Jesus promised the Samaritan woman an inner quenching, I abide in Your quiet water in my heart. Forgive me for being so easily distracted by other sources of empty promises and dry hopes. Draw me into Your presence again. Bring that sense of fulfillment that only You offer. Fill my soul.

A good shepherd knows the best waters for his sheep are quiet waters. Timid sheep need still water to drink from. Rapid currents can sweep a lamb into its flow and carry it away. As a father gives what's best for His children, you give only what's best for me. Thank You for Your still pool. Supply my needs.

You bring me to the water of Your choosing. Then You allow me to drink as much as I want. I feel sorry for those of Your sheep who choose to barely sip Your presence on Sunday morning. Their fear is that You'll take away something precious if they get too close. Calm my fears.

Grow my dependence on You so I imbibe Your very Being into my soul. Let me release my grip on this world and all it holds so I encounter You deeply. May this thirst I feel only be quenched by You. Help me choose that homesickness for heaven as my heart's desire. Slake my eternal thirst.

It's by the sacrifice of the Good Shepherd, Jesus Christ, I come to You now. Amen

PSALM 23:1A, 3A

The LORD is my shepherd, He restores my soul.

MATTHEW 11:28–30

Come to Me, all you who are weary and burdened, and I will give you rest. Take My yoke upon you and learn from Me, for I am gentle and humble in heart, and you will find rest for your souls. For My yoke is easy and My burden is light.

Dear Heavenly Father,

I struggle into Your presence from exhaustion. The weight of the world has beaten me down. I'm unsure how much longer I can go on. You come to me, carry me to Your throne of grace, and set me on Your lap. My head rests on Your strong shoulder as I gather energy from You. Thank You for understanding.

Rest, it feels like such a foreign concept in today's society. I wear a badge of honor when I'm tired from my efforts. That's not the way You designed me or this world. You even gave me Your example of rest in the very act of creation. You set aside an entire day to do nothing more than rest. Thank You for Your example.

It wasn't that You were tired from creating all I see from nothing. You're omnipotent. Your energy is inexhaustible. You could have kept making more, but You stopped when Your work was done. Grant me the wisdom to know when I need to step aside from my labors. My energy is exhaustible. Thank You for modeling.

I carry more burdens than You ever planned for me to tote. My worries weren't meant to be mine. Were they? Help me give control of my life back to You. I can't comprehend what You have in store for me. It's only after I see Your outcome that I understand Your wisdom. Thank You for directing.

Satan loves for me to carry more than I'm designed to bear. If he can keep me worn down, my efforts for You will be lessened. Guide my heart to focus on the tasks You have for me. Help me discard all those burdens You should be given. By this, my soul will indeed be restored. Thank You for restoring my soul.

It's by the One who is gentle and humble in heart, Jesus Christ, I come to You now. Amen

PSALM 23:1A, 3B

The LORD is my shepherd. He guides me in paths of righteousness for His name's sake.

Dear Heavenly Father,

I owe You an apology. I'm sorry I'm late. I got distracted coming to You. The urgent matters of this world so easily distract me from the important things of life. It's pitiful of me to give You the leftovers of my time and energy. Your love is displayed in Your hug once again. Your smile assures me You appreciate every second You can get from me. You're the best.

I need a guide to keep me on the right path. This world offers so many side streets and dead ends. Some people who were being used greatly by You have stumbled on those roads and didn't make it back on the best way. Stop me from following people who are fallible. Keep me in step with Jesus by studying Your word. You're my guide.

Your Word is a lamp to my feet. It shows me the next step to take. I too often want to see the whole course for my life. You know I can't handle more than the moment I'm in. Tomorrow will have its own troubles. Get me through today. The manna You provide is enough. Encourage me to take just the next step, then the next one. You're my provider.

Righteousness is such a foreign concept to me. I'm too sin-filled to attain it on my own. Jesus not only showed me the way by modeling righteousness; He built the bridge with His blood to help me be righteous in Your eyes. Only the righteous can be called Your adopted children. Thank You for choosing me, Father. You are gracious.

Only Your name is to be upheld above all others. I Am is I Am. The reason You keep me on the right path is for Your name alone. It isn't about me. It never was. It never should be. Maintain my focus on the goal of pleasing You. Bring me back to Your path quickly so I can keep You happy in all I do. You are glorious.

It's only because of the One I'll one day lay my crowns at His feet, Jesus Christ, I pray. Amen

PSALM 23:4A

Even though I walk through the valley of the shadow of death, I will fear no evil, for You are with me.

Dear Heavenly Father,

I squint at the light in Your presence. You wait with a smile for my eyes to adjust. I come to You in clear view. You have nothing to hide. Your love engulfs me before I reach Your embrace. I need those arms around me now. The comfort of Your security means everything to me. There's nothing to fear when I'm with You. Thank You for Your love.

My world is so dark and foreboding. The shadows I walk through are indeed intense. When my eyes are adjusted to these shadows, it's hard to see any light. Fear gets a grip on me, then worry and panic if I concentrate on the circumstances. Remind me of Your promise of hope and a future. You will never leave me nor forsake me. Thank You for Your promises.

There are many enemies that dog my steps. Death is a major one. I experience more than just physical death. The ending of a promised relationship leaves deep scars. The loss of a job can pull me into a grave of financial ruin. The limitations of declining health drain my will at times. A child making poor choices is heart-wrenching. Thank You for Your resurrection.

Give me the resolve to walk through each dark valley You have planned for me. Give me the courage to take the next step, especially when fear grips me. When the shadows overwhelm me, guide me by the Word I have hidden in my heart. Your Word is a lamp to my feet. With that, I can take the next step until I reach the end of the valley. Thank You for Your book.

The deepest valleys are found near the highest mountains. Not much is seen in the valley. The mountain tops hold an extremely different outlook. Grant me the strength to climb the hills of this life. Don't let me stay in the valleys. When I do experience physical death, it won't mean an ending but a glorious new beginning. Thank You for Your kingdom.

It's by the One who experienced the spiritual death I deserve, Jesus Christ, I pray. Amen

PSALM 23:1A, 4B

The Lord is my shepherd, His rod and
His staff, they comfort me.

Dear Heavenly Father,

I pause at the doorway to Your throne room. I'm ashamed to enter into Your perfect presence. I've done it again. I've blown it as Your witness. How will You treat me after such conduct? Your smile and outstretched arms beckon me to Your embrace once again. No one else would forgive me so openly. As I snuggle in, You give me a little tickle in my side. Help me receive Your grace.

I know I deserve Your rod of correction once again. I've felt it in the past by the consequences I still live with. If I hadn't insisted in getting my own way, I'd be better off today. Some lose positions in ministry by the actions of others who discover the truth. Some days it feels like the only thing I'm good at is making a mess of my life. Teach me wisdom from mistakes.

The shepherd's staff gives gentle coaxing for my life. A nudge from Your staff guides me back on track. You lift me by the hook in Your staff from the briers I step into when I wander away from You. How smooth my life runs when I listen to Your staff's guidance. It assures me that I belong to You even when I desert You. Give me guidance for life.

The discipline from Your rod shows Your love as much as the deliverance of Your staff. You are no complacent shepherd. You want what is best for me all the time. You know varying degrees of correction are needed throughout my life. Only a loving father cares enough to attempt to bend a strong will before destruction comes. Discipline me lovingly for betterment.

You have a plan for my mistakes. When I come out the other side and am closer to You, I have a duty to share my experience with others going through the same situation. They'll listen to someone who has gone down the same path as them. Use me to help another weary traveler who has lost their way. Utilize my experience for others.

It's by the Son who needed no discipline because He followed Your will perfectly, Jesus Christ, I pray. Amen

PSALM 23:1A, 5A

The Lord is my shepherd. He prepares a table before me in the presence of my enemies.

Dear Heavenly Father,

I glance over my shoulder before I come into your throne room. It feels like my enemies are close on my heels. When I turn to You, I see my enemies assembled. You are smiling as You set a meal out for me. A peace falls over me, a joy I know can only come from You. Help me remember You are much greater than anything this world throws at me. Your power is immense.

As I sit at the table, my enemies are silent. In Your presence, they are powerless. No harm will come to me that You don't allow first. They may be scheming their next opportunity, but now they are still. Discouragement folds his arms. Fear sits on his hands. Doubt drums his fingers on his leg. Lust twiddles her thumbs. Anger remains quiet. Your control is incredible.

Before I know it, the table is full with delicacies. Your lavishness is overwhelming. A simple sandwich is all I expected. The One who owns everything can't hold back from His adopted child.

You're so overjoyed to have me in Your presence You bring it all. The table expands to make room for more. I blush at all this attention. Your grace is amazing.

It's at times like this I wonder why I don't come to You more often. The excuses are so lame now. Surely others can wait while I soak in Your love. I can forgo a few minutes of sleep to be Your only child for a time each day. The urgent matters can wait while we deepen our relationship. I need to imbibe Your love letter to me more often. Your love is astounding.

Your perfect holiness is something I'll never attain while I walk this earth. But that doesn't mean I don't long to grasp as much of it as I can in this life. The only way a child can mimic a parent is to spend time with them. Take away this spirit of entitlement I have. Give me what You know I need in Your time. I too quickly become greedy. Your provision is enough.

It's by the name of Jesus Christ, the One who overcame the ultimate enemy, death, I can ever come to You. Amen

PSALM 23:1A, 5B

The LORD is my shepherd, He anoints my
head with oil; my cup overflows.

Dear Heavenly Father,

I come into Your throne room with my head bowed down. My self-worth is low today. How can one of such perfection want to be with me? I glance up and see Your smile. How quickly I forget You chose to adopt me. Your peace strengthens as I approach Your throne. You stop me when I'm at Your knees. Your acceptance is incredible.

Your smile broadens as You pull a flask out of Your robe. My head bows again, not in apprehension but in reverence. Every child of Yours is a joint heir with Jesus. Because of that, I require an anointing from You. It's not from my worth or anything I've done but Your decision alone. Your sanctifying is incomprehensible.

As the oil saturates my hair and scalp, the weight of responsibility increases. Becoming a ruler is no small task. I now see the purpose behind each of the trials and burdens of my life. Had I gotten my own way each time my eyes would never have opened to other's problems. Empathy is a great resource for a king. Your training is precise.

The value of Your anointing oil is priceless. I hold a cup below my head to capture every precious drop that falls from my scalp. I can't imagine wasting even one drop. Your anointing is so lavish my cup, which I thought would be ample, is soon flooding onto the floor. You surprise again by Your extravagance. Your resources are limitless.

As a shepherd uses oil to aid in the healing of wounds, I feel my own hurts mending. In Your presence, a comfort settles in. I pick up the cup at my feet and head out to comfort others going through the same hurt. Use me to reach people with the fact of Your love and acceptance for all who believe. Your grace is amazing.

It's by the Son in whom You are well pleased, Jesus Christ, I come to You now. Amen

PSALM 23:6

Surely goodness and love will follow me
all the days of my life, and I will dwell in
the house of the LORD forever.

Dear Heavenly Father,

I run into Your throne room and climb on Your lap. Your smile and embrace are as warm as ever. I'm so glad we have this time together. I can't imagine getting through life without it. The demands of this world will pull me out of here for a time. But, one day, this will never end. When my time on earth is done, we'll share time forever. Thank You for this promise.

When I step into the world I live in, the contrast is sharp. So many people are living for the momentary pleasure they find. They have no eternal hope. They haven't been properly introduced to Your goodness and love. Use me to let them know You. May the good and love You possess reflect off me. Thank You for this possibility.

Your goodness uses all the events in my life to mold me into the image of Jesus Christ. Your love compels me to reach out to the hurting without expecting anything in return. My focus is on Your kingdom, not my happiness at the expense of others. As Your adopted child, You promise to stay with me as my Father. Thank You for this potential.

Just before Jesus left this earth, He stated he had to leave. Another mission awaited Him. He had to go back to the carpentry trade in heaven. He's building homes for Your adopted children for when our time on earth is done. I long for that time of no more pain, or tears, or separation from You. Thank You for this program.

Until then, I have a battle to fight. Jesus also gave a commission to me before He left. I must make disciples. I must feed others Your truth and love as He did. Supply me the strength, wisdom, fortitude, and desire to fight the good fight for Your kingdom. Keep my focus on You as I meet the needs I see around me. Thank You for this provision.

It's only and always because of Jesus and all He accomplished while on earth I can even come to You. Amen

PRAYER TOPICS

TOPIC	PAGE NUMBER	TOPIC	PAGE NUMBER
Abiding in Christ	144	Faith	20, 100, 170
Adultery	122	Fear	202, 220
Anger	70	Forgiveness	72
		Fulfillment	184
Bible	24		
Blessing	190	General	28, 106
Boasting	62	Gentleness	102
Boldness	194, 198	God's Will	200
Bread	132	Goodness	98
Coveting	128	Hate	164
Creation	172	Healing	152
Death	150, 220	Homesickness	186, 228
		Hope	80, 186
Dependence	214		
Discipline	212, 222	I AM	147
		Idolatry	112
Emptiness	182		
Envy	60	Joy	90
Failure	84	Judgment	156, 178, 200

TOPIC	PAGE NUMBER	TOPIC	PAGE NUMBER
Killing	152	Provision	224
Kindness	58, 96	Purity	42
Laughter	154	Rapture	176
Life	140, 142	Rest	116, 216
Light	52, 134	Reverence	202, 206
Love	88, 164	Righteousness	16, 38, 174, 218
Lying	126	Rudeness	66
Mercy	40		
Mourning	34, 154	Salt	50
Murder	120	Salvation	22, 142
		Self-control	104
Needs	210	Selfishness	68
		Shepherd	138
Obedience	110, 180, 188	Stealing	124
Parents	118	Surrender	10
Patience	56, 94	Swearing	114
Peace	18, 44, 92, 166		
Persecution	46, 48	Trials	226
Perseverance	82, 204	Trust	78, 192, 194
		Truth	14, 74, 142
Pleasure	196		
Power/meekness	36	War	166
Prayer	26	Weeping	154
Pride	64	Wisdom	160, 162
Priorities	158		
Protection	76, 136		

www.ingramcontent.com/pod-product-compliance
Lightning Source LLC
Chambersburg PA
CBHW020138130526
44591CB00030B/116